pastry

pastry

RICHARD BERTINET

Contents

About the author   6

Introduction   8

1   The Pastries   10

2   Salted   64

3   Sweet   102

4   Puff   148

5 Choux   178

6 Finishing Touches   196

Suppliers   213

Index   216

Online resources   215

Acknowledgements   223

About the author

Originally from Brittany, Richard Bertinet trained as a baker from the age of 14. Having moved to the UK in the 1980s, he is now very much an Anglophile.

With 20 years' experience in the kitchen, baking, consulting and teaching, Richard moved to Bath in 2005 to open The Bertinet Kitchen cookery school. The school attracts people from all over the world to participate in Richard's classes and has been highly praised, including recognition by US Gourmet magazine and the television series Adventures with Ruth [Reichl], in which it featured as one of the best cookery schools in the world.

As well as instilling passion through his teaching, Richard works as a consultant for major manufacturers developing speciality products throughout the industry.

The Bertinet Bakery started life as a weekly pop-up shop above the cookery school in 2007 but has grown to a much larger affair producing breads and pastries for restaurants, hotels and food stores in the South West and supplying the bakery's own shops in Bath with more to come further afield. The bakery's signature sourdough loaf was the winner of the Soil Association's award for Best Baked Good in 2010 and 2011.

Richard's first book *Dough* received a host of accolades including the Guild of Food Writers' Best First Book Award, the Julia Child Award for Best First Book, a James Beard Award for Best Book Baking & Desserts and the International Association of Culinary Professionals Cookery Book of the Year Award. His second book Crust was also published to critical acclaim and received a World Gourmand Award. His third book, *COOK*, focused on many of the dishes taught at the cookery school.

Richard was named as the BBC Food Champion of the Year 2010 at the BBC Food & Farming Awards.

For more information about Richard, The Bertinet Kitchen and The Bertinet Bakery visit www.bertinet.com

Introduction

When I wrote my first book, *Dough*, my aim was to show people that bread-making is for everyone, and should be fun, not daunting and complicated, which has been the previous experience of many people who come to my classes at the Bertinet Kitchen. Now this book aims to do the same for pastry, because I realise that people are often just as scared of making pastry as bread. There is an idea that some people are just naturally good pastry-makers, or that you can only make great pastry if you have cold hands. I don't believe that. Anyone can make fantastic pastry, and I will show you how.

Along the way I will also talk you through resting and rolling pastry, and baking blind. This last technique simply involves baking a pastry case in the oven without a filling, but the idea seems to cause a lot of confusion. I am constantly asked: Why do you do it? How brown should the pastry be? If you bake it blind, then put in a filling and bake it for another half hour or so, will the pastry burn? How do you stop the pastry from cracking and shrinking in the oven? I will answer all these questions and many more.

One of the reasons that pastry-making can seem challenging is that there are so many different names you are likely to come across, from shortcrust to sweet shortcrust or rich shortcrust, puff, rough puff, pâte brisée, pâte feuilletée, flaky, choux, suet and hot-water crust. My advice is not to worry about most of these. When you start baking at home, you don't need to master a dozen different kinds of pastry in order to make beautiful pies and tarts to feed the family and impress your friends. Like anything you learn in life, it makes sense to get the basics right and build your confidence, then you can become more adventurous later on. So for this book I have narrowed everything down to just four main categories of pastry, and devoted a chapter to each type.

I call the principal ones simply 'salted' and 'sweet' because these are the names we used in the bakery where I did my apprenticeship in my native France: 'salé' (meaning salted) for the savoury pastry (not because it contains a lot of salt), and 'sucrée' (literally sugared) for the sweet pastry. It was so straightforward. These are the all-purpose shortcrust pastries that you can use for any pie or open tart, and they are made using the same method.

As I have said, I try to keep things simple, but at the end of the Salted chapter I have added a recipe for pork pies made with hot-water crust, which is a pastry used only for making raised pies, the kind you eat cold. I have included it because most people I know love pork pies, but think they are tricky to make because traditionally they are 'hand raised', i.e. the pastry casing is formed by hand. My recipe is very straightforward and offers a much easier way of making the pies.

The fourth and fifth chapters are about pastries that are both light and airy, but have different characteristics and involve two very different techniques. Puff pastry is all about rolling and folding to create layers with air trapped between them so that in the oven this air expands and the pastry literally puffs up (think of cream slices or vol-au-vents). By contrast, choux pastry, which is used for things such as profiteroles, involves making a 'batter' with the texture of very thick custard. The moisture in the dough creates steam in the heat of the oven and puffs out the pastry, making it quite hollow and airy.

These four pastries are all you need to start to create a wealth of tarts and pies, and even biscuits. And I also explain how to present and decorate fruit tarts in the artistic way that makes the displays in French bakeries look so stunning.

Just as *Dough* encouraged everyone to make bread-making part of the routine of feeding family and friends, I hope that this book will do the same for pastry, and that by keeping things simple and starting from just four key recipes, you can relax, enjoy yourself, bake with confidence, and perhaps even show off a little bit.

1   The Pastries

In this chapter I explain how to make four basic pastries – salted, sweet, puff and choux, which are all you need to make the recipes in chapters 2–5, and to make virtually any other pastry dish you can think of. It's a good idea always to make at least double quantities of salted, sweet and puff pastry and freeze what you don't use, so you will always have some pastry on hand to make a comforting pie or an impressive-looking tart.

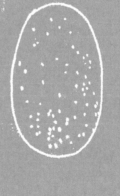

Sizes, Weights and Measures

Throughout the book all eggs are medium and all spoon measures are level unless stated otherwise.

Like all bakers and pastry-makers, I am a stickler for weighing ingredients because baking is all about being precise and consistent. If you are making a casserole, it really doesn't matter if you use more carrots than parsnips, or a whole bottle of wine rather than half, but if you were to be that loose with your ingredients when you are baking, you would have a disaster on your hands. So when I am making pastry I weigh everything, including water, because weighing is more accurate than judging the level in a measuring jug. I know it sounds pedantic, and you can use millilitres if you prefer, but in my classes I encourage people to be as accurate as possible so that they get the best and most consistent results.

Likewise, although I have given the quantity of salt for the pastry recipes in terms of teaspoons, there are so many different sizes of teaspoon that I prefer to weigh out 5 grams. With modern scales, weighing small quantities like this isn't a problem.

Ovens

....

A word about ovens, as I am always being asked what type I use at our bakery and cooking school. Well, we use domestic fan ovens, just as people would have at home. The heat is more consistent at top and bottom, which helps to give more even baking. That said, if you have a good static oven, you will get equally good results.

Many recipe books give different temperatures for static and fan ovens, but the ethos of this book is to keep everything as simple and unambiguous as possible, so I give only Centigrade temperatures and Gas marks, which can be used for either static or fan ovens. The reality is that 10 degrees either way shouldn't make a dramatic difference to your baking. Also, the only way to bake with complete confidence is to get to know your oven. It might give you perfectly uniform heat, on the other hand it might have hotspots or be slightly hotter or cooler than the dial indicates.

Every oven is different, which makes it difficult to write foolproof baking recipes that will work for every oven in every kitchen in the country. In my classes I always suggest that the first time you use a recipe, you don't take the baking time as gospel. I have a 'five minute rule', which means check every five minutes, as a tart that bakes in 20 minutes in my oven might need only 15 minutes, or up to 25, in yours. There is no substitute for keeping an eye on whatever you are baking and, if necessary, moving baking trays and tins higher or lower, or turning them around if you feel one side is colouring more quickly than the other.

After a while you will get to know the way your oven behaves, and be able to adjust the temperature a little one way or another to suit. Even better, it is worth investing in a good oven thermometer to find out what the temperature actually is in different parts of your oven.

Salted and Sweet Pastry

It is a myth that you need cold hands to make good salted or sweet pastry, but you do need cold butter and a quick, light touch. It is squeezing and overworking that heats up the pastry and makes it greasy and sticky, not the temperature of your hands. In my classes people are always amazed that I leave the butter in the fridge until I am ready to use it, as most pastry recipes call for softened butter. Then what happens is that, unless you have planned ahead, the temptation is to put the butter into the microwave to soften it quickly, and it melts from the inside and turns oily, which makes your pastry even more likely to be greasy. The key is to keep the butter very cold but still soft and pliable, and I will show you how in the method beginning on page 18.

Although you can mix pastry by machine, doing it by hand is such a quick and easy process that I suggest you do it that way, at least at first if you are new to making pastry. Even if you move on to using a machine later, you will get the feel of what you are looking for in terms of texture, and be more in control of the machine. Besides, you still need to finish the dough off by hand once it is mixed.

There was a time when pastry recipes always began by telling you to sift the flour, but nowadays there is usually no need to because the modern milling process sifts the flour so many times that it will flow quite freely and have no lumps. The only time I sift flour is when making choux pastry because this helps incorporate it more swiftly and smoothly into the mixture of boiling water and butter. (For the same reason I would also sift the flour when making a sponge cake, as the flour needs to be quickly folded in at the last minute.)

Once you are comfortable with making salted and sweet pastry, you can vary the flavours in any number of ways, perhaps replacing some of the plain flour with wholemeal or semolina flour, adding caraway seeds, chocolate or the zest and juice of a lemon. For some of the recipes I have suggested using a particular one of these flavoured pastries, but you can experiment as much as you like.

Salted pastry

This recipe makes 420 g of pastry dough, and each of the recipes in the Salted chapter uses one quantity of it. This is enough dough for any of the following tin sizes:

- 24 tartlets made in 12-hole tins
- 8 individual tarts made in 10 cm loose-bottomed tins (2 cm deep)
- 1 large tart, made in a 26 cm loose-bottomed tin or ring (4 cm deep)

These sizes are what I use in my kitchen, but don't worry if your tins and rings are slightly different. And naturally, you can use whatever shape of tin or ring you like: just keep an eye on your tarts and pies while they bake as you might need to adjust the time in the oven (see page 13). If you don't need all the pastry, you can freeze what is left (see page 63).

250 g plain flour
5 g (1 tsp) salt
125 g butter, straight from the fridge
1 egg
35 g or ml cold water

Salted pastry variations

Wholemeal pastry: Use wholemeal flour instead of the plain flour.
You might need an extra tablespoon of water.
Spelt pastry: Substitute 125 g of the plain flour with wholemeal spelt flour.
(If using white spelt flour, substitute all the plain flour with this.)
Semolina pastry: Substitute 50 g of the plain flour with semolina flour or polenta, and add a pinch of turmeric.
Cornish pasty pastry: Use margarine instead of butter.
Caraway pastry: Add 4 teaspoons caraway seeds to the flour.

Sweet pastry

This recipe makes 720 g of pastry dough, and each of the recipes in the Sweet chapter uses one quantity of it. This is enough dough for any of the following tin sizes:

* 36 tartlets made in 12-hole tins
* 24 slightly larger tartlets made in 8 cm loose-bottomed tins or rings (2 cm deep)
* 12 individual tarts made in 10 cm loose-bottomed tins or rings (2 cm deep)
* 4 larger tarts, made in 16 cm loose-bottomed tins or rings (2 cm deep)
* 2 large tarts made in 20 cm loose-bottomed tins or rings (4 cm deep)
* 1 large tart made in a 26 cm loose-bottomed tin (4 cm deep), with enough left over to make smaller tarts of your choice.

The recipes in the Sweet chapter use quite a range of tins as I find that different fruits and toppings lend themselves visually to particular sizes, but remember, the sizes given are just a guide. Feel free to use whatever size or shape of tins and rings you have, but keep checking while the tarts are in the oven as you might need to adjust the baking time (see page 13). If you don't need all the pastry, you can freeze what is left (see page 63).

350 g flour
125 g butter
125 g sugar
2 eggs plus one yolk
pinch of salt

Sweet pastry variations

Chocolate pastry: Add 20 g cocoa with the flour.
Almond pastry: Use only 250 g flour and add 100 g ground almonds with the flour.
Hazelnut and almond pastry: Use only 275 g flour and add 30 g hazelnuts,
50 g flaked almonds and 100 g ground almonds with the flour.
Pistachio pastry: Use only 250 g flour and add 100 g ground pistachio nuts with the flour.
Lemon pastry: Add the zest of a lemon and the juice of half of it when you add the eggs.

To make the dough by hand

Measure out all your ingredients before you start, and break your egg(s) into a small bowl – there is no need to beat them. If making sweet pastry, separate the remaining egg. Put the flour and salt into a mixing bowl.

Now for the cold butter. What I do is take it straight from the fridge and put it between two pieces of greaseproof paper or butter wrappers (I always keep butter wrappers to use for this, as well as for greasing tins and rings), then bash it firmly with a rolling pin.

The idea is to soften it while still keeping it cold. I end up with a thin, cold slab about a centimetre thick that bends like plasticine. Put the whole slab into the bowl of flour – there is no need to chop it up.

Cover the butter well with flour and tear it into large pieces.

Now it's time to flake the flour and butter together – this is where you want a really light touch. With both hands, scoop up the flour-covered butter and flick your thumbs over the surface, pushing away from you, as if you are dealing a pack of cards.

You need just a soft, skimming motion – no pressing or squeezing – and the butter will quickly start to break into smaller pieces. Keep plunging your hands into the bowl, and continue with the light flicking action, making sure all the pieces of butter remain coated with flour so they don't become sticky.

The important thing now is to stop mixing when the shards of butter are the size of your little fingernail. There is an idea that you have to keep rubbing in the butter until the mixture looks like breadcrumbs, but you don't need to take it that far. When people come to my classes, I find they can't resist putting their hands back into the bowl to rub it just a little bit more, but if you want a light pastry, it is really important not to overwork it. If the mixture starts to get sticky now, imagine how much worse it will be when you start to add the liquid at the next stage. If you are making sweet pastry, add the sugar at this point, mixing it in evenly.

Tip the egg(s), and the extra yolk if making sweet pastry, into the flour mixture, add the water (salted pastry only) and mix everything together.

You can mix with a spoon, but I prefer to use one of the little plastic scrapers that I use for bread-making. Because it is bendy, it's very easy to scrape around the sides of the bowl and pull the mixture into the centre until it forms a very rough dough that shouldn't be at all sticky.

While it is still in the bowl, press down on the dough with both thumbs, then turn the dough clockwise a few degrees and press down and turn again. Repeat this a few times.

With the help of your spoon or scraper, turn the pastry onto a work surface.

Work the dough as you did when it was in the bowl: holding the dough with both hands, press down gently with your thumbs, then turn the dough clockwise a few degrees, press down with your thumbs again and turn. Repeat this about four or five times in all.

Now fold the pastry over itself and press down with your fingertips. Provided the dough isn't sticky, you shouldn't need to flour the surface, but if you do, make sure you give it only a really light dusting, not handfuls, as this extra flour will all go into your pastry and make it heavier.

When you flour your work surface, you need to do this as if you are skimming a stone over water, just paying out a light spray of flour. (Funny as it seems, people in my classes actually practise this, like a new sport.) You need just enough to create a filmy barrier so that you can glide the pastry around the work surface without it sticking.

Repeat the folding and pressing down with your fingertips a couple of times until the dough is like plasticine, and looks homogeneous.

Finally, pick up the piece of pastry and tap each side on the work surface to square it off so that when you come to roll it, you are starting off with a good shape rather than raggedy edges.

To make the dough with a food mixer

Put the flour and salt into the bowl of the machine. Bash the butter as described in the hand-mixing method, then break it into four or five pieces and add it to the flour. Using a paddle attachment rather than a hook or whisk, mix the ingredients at a slow speed until the pieces of butter are about the size of your little fingernail. You will need to scrape the butter from the paddle a few times as it will stick. If you are making sweet pastry, add the sugar at this point and mix in well. Add the egg(s), and yolk (if making sweet pastry) and water (if making salted pastry) and mix very briefly, until a dough forms. As soon as it does, turn it out onto your work surface with the help of your scraper and follow the hand-mixing method.

To make the dough with a food processor

It is very easy to overwork pastry in a food processor, so be very careful. Put the flour and salt into the bowl of the machine. Cut the cold butter into small dice and add to the bowl. Use the pulse button in short bursts so that the flour just lifts and mixes, lifts and mixes. You don't want to blitz everything into a greasy ball as that will result in hard, dense pastry. If you are making sweet pastry, add the sugar at this point and mix in well. Add the egg(s), and yolk (if making sweet pastry) and water (if making salted pastry), then pulse briefly until the pastry dough comes together. Turn it out with the help of your scraper and follow the hand-mixing method.

Resting the pastry

Wrap the pastry in greaseproof paper, *not* cling film, which will make it sweaty, and rest it in the fridge for at least 1 hour, preferably several, or, better still, overnight. The reason you rest pastry is that it helps the gluten in the flour to relax so that the pastry becomes more elastic and easier to roll. It also helps to prevent shrinkage later when it goes in the oven.

If you are really in a hurry to use the pastry, flatten it to about half its depth with a rolling pin before wrapping it in greaseproof as this will allow it to chill more quickly. Alternatively, put it into the freezer for 15–30 minutes.

Choosing tart tins and rings

Some of the recipes in this book use 12-hole tartlet tins; others use tins with loose bases, or rings and squares that are simply placed on a baking tray.

Even if you're using loose-bottomed tins, it is best to put these on top of a baking tray rather than straight onto the oven shelf, partly in case the filling leaks, but mainly because it is much easier to move them around and take out of the oven, especially if you are wearing oven gloves.

It's preferable to use non-stick tins and rings. After baking, I wipe all of mine, whether non-stick or not, with a clean tea towel – I try not to wash them or put them in the dishwasher, and am careful not to scratch the non-stick ones with anything sharp. Then, before using them, I rub them very lightly with butter (butter wrappers are best for this), or spray with a little baking spray (again, I do this even if I am using non-stick tins or rings, just in case). If you are going to be baking the next day, you can do this greasing before storing the tins and rings away (that is what I do) so that they are ready to go straight away.

Rolling out

The secret of a great pie or tart is to get the right balance of pastry and filling so that neither dominates. The more you bake, the more you will get a feeling for this, but for the recipes in this book I suggest you use a simple guideline. For small tarts and pies up to and including 10 cm in diameter (or the equivalent square/rectangular shape), roll out the pastry 2–3 mm thick. For larger tarts and pies, roll out the pastry 5 mm thick. Remember, if you're not using all of the pastry straight away, you can divide it up and freeze some of it at this point (see page 63).

Lightly dust your work surface with flour (see page 24), then move the pastry around to coat it. Lightly flour your rolling pin too. Keeping your fingers on the outer ends of the pin, roll it backwards and forwards in short, sharp movements without pressing down too hard on the pastry or stretching it.

Keep lifting the pastry up after every two rolls, and move it through a quarter turn to get some air underneath it and stop it from sticking to the work surface. Continue rolling until it is the size and thickness required for your recipe, and large enough to leave an overhang when you line your tin or ring.

Roll the pastry around your rolling pin so that you can lift it up without stretching it.

Lining tart tins and rings

To line a 12-hole tin, or 8 cm loose-bottomed tartlet tins, use a circular cutter or upturned glass to stamp out circles of pastry about 2.5 cm bigger than the holes or, in the case of individual tins, about 3 cm bigger to allow for the depth and leave a little bit of overhang.

If using tins with unusual shapes, such as the leaf ones pictured, place one of them upside down on the pastry and cut around it, again leaving a border of about 3 cm. To line larger tins or rings (over 8 cm in diameter), make sure you roll out your circle or square of pastry large enough to cover the depth of the tin or ring and leave about 2.5 cm overhang.

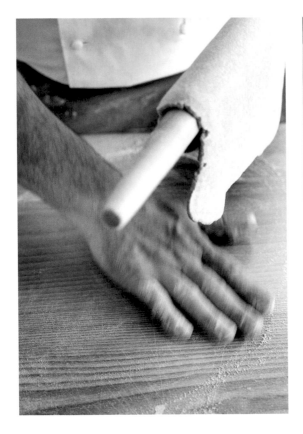 

Lift your rolling pin with the pastry wrapped around it.

Holding the pin at each end, drape the pastry over whatever tin or ring you are using.

Let the pastry fall inside, easing it gently and carefully down into the base and sides without pulling or stretching it.

Leave the pastry overhanging the edges of your tin or ring. If using fluted tins, press the pastry lightly into the shaped sides.

Once your tin is lined, tap it lightly against the work surface to settle in the pastry. If using a ring, just lift up the baking tray it is sitting on and tap it down. If you are going to blind bake the pastry, see the relevant steps on pages 37–42. Otherwise, put the lined tin or ring in the fridge for at least 30 minutes (or in the freezer for 15 minutes). This will help to stop the pastry from cracking, shrinking and pulling away from the edges when it is later put in the oven.

Remove the pastry case(s) from the fridge. The pastry overhang on large tins can be left in place and removed with a sharp knife just before serving. If you are using small tins, trim the pastry around the edges with a knife *before* filling and baking as trimming will be tricky to do once the tarts are baked. (Provided the pastry has rested for long enough, it shouldn't shrink.) If the tins are fluted you might find it easier to carefully tear away the excess with your fingers.

Heating the oven

It sounds obvious but make sure you turn your oven on in plenty of time so that it is properly hot when you're ready to bake – you don't want your beautifully chilled pastry to sit around getting warm while you wait for the oven to reach the right temperature. One of the secrets of avoiding the dreaded 'soggy bottom' and achieving a good crisp finish to your tarts and pies is to get the heat to the base immediately. As a baker, I always have a hot baking stone, which is actually a piece of granite, in my oven – so every time I switch it on it heats up. In my classes I always suggest people get the same effect at home by using the grill pan and turning it upside down. Then all you have to do is place the tray holding your tin or tins straight onto it. If you're baking more than will fit on the grill pan, you can always put in an upturned baking tray on a separate shelf.

Baking blind

There is a great deal of confusion about blind baking, and I find it helps to explain that blind baking is not *part* baking, it is *pre*-baking. Baking blind is simply a way of fully baking a pastry case, large or small, without a filling so that you can use it as you wish – putting in something cold and ready to eat, such as fruit and cream, or adding a liquid filling, such as crème fraîche, eggs and bacon, that needs to be cooked and set. I know people worry that returning a baked pastry case to the oven for another 30 minutes or so after it is filled will result in burnt pastry, but once the filling is put in, unless the tarts are very tiny, the temperature in the oven is turned down, and the pastry won't colour any more, except around the overhanging edges, which will be trimmed off anyway.

Why bake blind if you are going to put the case back in the oven anyway? You do this either because the filling will be set in a shorter time than it takes to fully bake the pastry, or because the filling is very liquid. Think about a mixture for quiche: when you put it in it is quite runny, and even though it will take around the same time to cook as it would for the pastry to bake, the pastry actually has no chance of crisping up with all that wet filling on top. The result: soggy bottom pastry.

I think it helps to understand the principle of what actually happens when you blind bake. You do it in two stages. First, to help the pastry hold its shape when it goes into the oven, you line it with baking paper filled with baking beans. Then, once the pastry has begun to dry out and keep its shape, you take it out of the oven, brush it with beaten egg (egg wash) and put it back in the oven to form a hard seal that is fully 'waterproof' so the pastry will stay crisp, whatever you put into it.

It's always worth holding on to leftover pastry, even if it's just scraps, because, if you are baking blind, these can be used to patch up any broken pastry cases before they're brushed with egg wash and put back in the oven. Of course, if you have rolled and rested your pastry properly, there won't be any holes or cracks, I hope.

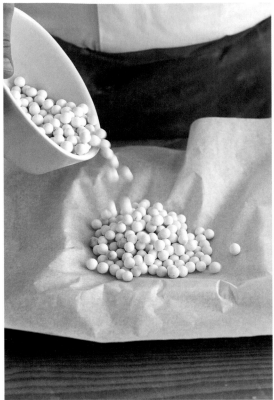

Blind baking loose-bottomed tins and rings

First, prick the base of the pastry all over with a fork. This stops it from rising up when in the oven (even though it will also be held down by baking beans, it can sometimes manage to lift a little). Unless you are making small tartlets (up to 8 cm), don't trim the pastry. Leave it overhanging the edge.

Place a large sheet of baking paper over the top of the pastry case, then tip in ceramic baking beans and spread them out so that they completely cover the base. (Traditionally dried beans or peas were used for this, and are fine, but the ceramic ones can be kept in a container and used over and over again.) Put the lined tin in the fridge for 30 minutes (or the freezer for 15 minutes) to rest and relax.

Preheat the oven to the temperature specified in the recipe. Bake small tarts and pies (10 cm or less) for 15 minutes, and larger ones for 20 minutes. As I mentioned on page 13 in my classes when people ask me how long to bake for, I say, 'Five minutes!' Of course they look at me as if I'm crazy, but I explain that I want to get everyone in the habit of keeping an eye on pastry in the oven. If I were to say 20 minutes, in their minds they would just switch off and forget about it for that length of time. But baking times are only a reference, not to be taken as gospel, especially when you are new to baking and not quite sure how your oven behaves. (There is no uniformity where ovens are concerned.) So have a look after five minutes, then after another five minutes, then...

When the base of the pastry has dried out and is very lightly coloured, like parchment, remove it from the oven and lift out the baking paper and beans. Don't worry if the overhanging edges are quite brown, as you will be trimming these away after you have finished baking your tart. Have ready some beaten egg (I add a pinch of salt as this breaks down the egg and makes it easier to spread with a pastry brush. It also makes the colour look darker so don't worry, this is normal.) Brush this over the inside of the pastry case to seal it. Hopefully, there should be no cracks or holes, but if there are, don't panic. Just take a tiny scrap of leftover pastry, dip it into your beaten egg and use your finger to rub it over the crack, as if you were putting filler in a wall. Return the tin to the oven.

 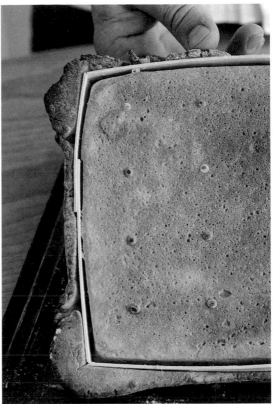

Small cases need another 8 minutes, and larger ones a further 10 minutes. If you have done a little bit of patching, the extra dough will be so thin that it will bake in this time, and once the pastry case is filled, no one will ever know. The inside of the pastry will now be quite a dark golden brown and shiny from the egg glaze.

If you turn the tart case over, the base should also be well browned and crispy.

Blind baking a 12-hole tin

The easiest way to blind bake a 12-hole tin is simply to put an identical (empty) tin on top, but first grease the base very lightly with butter or a non-stick baking spray. Then put something like an ovenproof dish on top to weigh it down. Bake for the time stated in the recipe, then remove the baking dish and top tray. Brush the inside of the pastry cases with beaten egg and return to the oven for the time given in the recipe. Alternatively, 12-hole tins can be baked blind in exactly the same way as individual tins and rings, using baking paper and beans.

Puff pastry

I really hope that when you have the time, you will have a go at making puff pastry, as it is very satisfying. However, I know that it is a long process, and even when you have mastered the technique and got into the habit of making it in big batches so that you can keep some in the freezer, there will inevitably be a day when you have none left and no time to make more. Since the whole point of this book is to encourage more people to have a go at baking and enjoy themselves while doing it, I would much rather you used a good, ready-made puff pastry than not bake at all. There are some really good all-butter puff pastries out there, and it is worth keeping a supply in the freezer – hopefully alongside your own homemade pastry.

Puff pastry differs from others in that you make it by constantly rolling and folding the dough so that you create lots of layers or 'leaves' with air trapped in between. (The French name for this pastry is *feuilletée*, which means 'leafy'.) In the heat of the oven these air pockets expand, so the layers separate and the pastry as a whole puffs up.

The more rolling and folding you do, the more layers you create. Each series of foldings is known as a 'turn', and six turns is the ideal. These are easy to achieve in bakeries, where they have an automatic rolling pin called a pastry brake. At home, though, quite a bit of time and effort is involved, as you need to put the pastry back into the fridge after each turn so that it is always cold to work with. The first few times you make it, I suggest you do three double turns instead of six single ones, as explained below. In bakeries this is known as a 'double book'.

This recipe makes about 500 g of pastry, but I find it is much easier to make puff pastry in large amounts, so I always suggest making double the quantity, and then putting whatever you don't need into the freezer so you will always have some 'ready to go' (see page 63).

250 g plain flour

5 g (1 tsp) salt

100 g or ml cold water

juice of ¼ lemon

200 g unsalted butter, straight from the fridge

Have the flour and salt in a bowl, and the water in a jug. Squeeze the lemon juice into the water at the last minute. (The juice helps stop the pastry from becoming dark during the long folding and resting process.)

Gradually add the water and lemon juice, mixing with a scraper or spoon until you have a rough dough.

Turn the dough onto your work surface and knead it by folding it onto itself, then pressing down with your fingertips or the heel of your hand. The important thing is to stop just as it comes together – this will take about 2 minutes – then shape it quickly into a rough ball.

Now you need to make two deep cuts in the shape of a cross on top of the dough, then open it out a little and lift it into a bowl. Cut open a freezer bag, lay it loosely over the top, then rest it in the fridge or a very cool place for 1 hour.

Very lightly dust your work surface with flour (see page 24) and sit your rested dough on it. Gently ease out each of the four corners of the dough.

Then roll it out, just until it forms a square of roughly 20 cm. Place your cold butter between two sheets of greaseproof paper and bash with a rolling pin (see page 18). You want the butter to be a smaller square shape than your dough, about 2 cm smaller all round (i.e. roughly 18 cm). Lift off the top sheet of greaseproof paper, then turn the butter over onto the centre of the dough so that it is at a 45-degree angle to it (i.e. its straight sides are opposite the corners) and remove the remaining sheet of greaseproof (see picture opposite). Doing this means that you don't touch the butter directly, so you avoid warming it up.

Fold each side of the dough over the butter to enclose it completely in a parcel. This is the crucial part of the process as you need to make sure there are no gaps where the butter could seep through.

Gently, using your rolling pin, make dents all the way across the parcel to squash the butter a little inside (see picture opposite). Now roll out the pastry lightly and gently, lengthways only, into a rectangle 2–3 times longer than its original length. (It's important to do this lightly as if you press down hard on the dough, you run the risk of the butter warming up and seeping out, and the pastry will become heavy. Each time you roll, lift the dough a little and move it around slightly to get some air underneath it and help stop it from sticking.

Double book

Turn the dough so the long side of the rectangle is nearest you. Fold in the two ends to meet in the middle, then fold them over again. With your finger, make a dimple in the top of the dough to indicate that this is the first turn. This is an old bakery trick – very handy if you go off and do something else, then forget how many turns you have given the dough. Put the dough on a tray, cover loosely with an opened-out freezer bag and leave to rest in the fridge for 20–30 minutes.

Lightly flour your work surface and place the rested dough on it with the short end facing you. Roll it again lengthways, then turn it so that the long side is nearest you and fold as before. This time make two dimples on the top to indicate the second folding, and again rest in the fridge for 20–30 minutes. Repeat this rolling and resting process once more. The pastry is now ready to use.

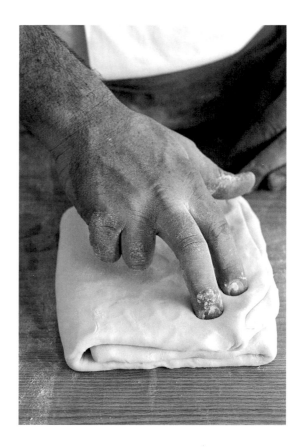

Single turn

Once you are more experienced, you can try doing six single turns rather than the double book described on page 53. Place the pastry with the long edge nearest you, but this time fold in just one side, then fold the other side over the top. With your finger, make a dimple in the top of the dough to remind yourself that this is the first turn. Put on a tray, cover loosely with an opened-out freezer bag and leave to rest in the fridge for 20–30 minutes.

Lightly flour your work surface and place the rested dough on it with the short end nearest you. Roll it again lengthways, then turn it so that the long side is nearest you and fold as before. This time make two dimples on the top to indicate the second turn, and again rest it in the fridge for 20–30 minutes. Repeat this rolling, folding and resting process until you have done six turns in all, marking the top of the dough each time with the appropriate number of dimples. The pastry is now ready to use.

Choux pastry

Although this is a type of puffed pastry, it is made using a completely different but very simple technique that involves boiling up water and butter in a pan, whisking in the flour and then beating in the eggs to create a batter the consistency of thick custard. This expands in the oven, leaving a light, airy centre.

As I mentioned earlier, while I don't sift flour for making salted or sweet pastry, I *do* sift it when making choux pastry as this helps to incorporate the flour more quickly and smoothly into the boiling water and butter.

125 g plain flour

225 g or ml water

60 g butter

½ tsp salt

4 eggs

Have all your ingredients ready before you start. Sift the flour into a mixing bowl. Bring the water, butter and salt to the boil in a large pan.

Tip in the flour in a steady stream.

Keep whisking all the time until the mixture clings to the whisk.

Swap the whisk for a wooden spoon and beat well over the heat for 2–3 minutes, until the mixture is glossy and comes away from the edges of the pan. This hard cooking dries off the batter, ready to take the eggs.

 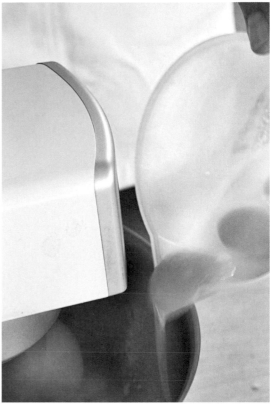

Because the mixture is quite hard to work by hand, I would use a food mixer, if possible. Beat the mixture with a paddle attachment for a minute.

Now start to add the eggs one at a time while keeping the motor running. If you prefer to beat in the eggs by hand, transfer the mixture to a bowl and beat them in one by one with a wooden spoon. Whether mixing by hand or machine, go carefully with the eggs as you might not need them all. You are aiming for a mixture that is smooth and glossy but that will hold its shape for piping. When you reach that point, it is ready to use.

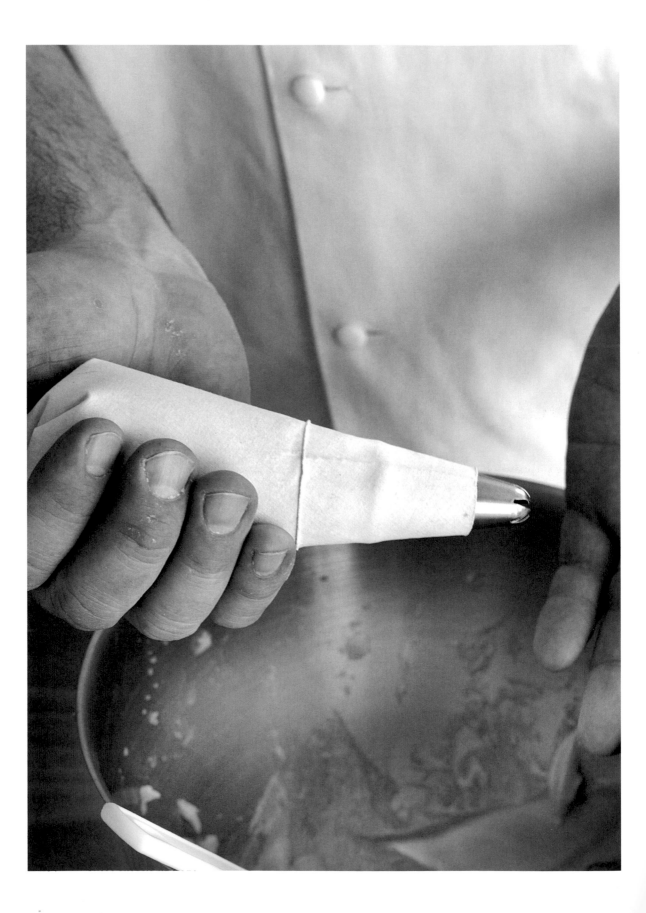

Piping Bags

Of course you can spoon choux batter onto your greased baking trays in little mounds or strips, to make buns or éclairs, but it is much more controllable if you pipe it, and you will need to do this if you want to make the classic choux swans on page 181. Like any other baking skill, piping is about technique and practice – and once you get the hang of it, it is very simple and satisfying to do.

Although you can buy very good disposable piping bags, I prefer the fabric ones because you can get a better grip on them as you pipe. The drawback is that they need to be washed out very carefully with hot soapy water, rinsed and then hung up to dry somewhere warm, such as near the oven, once they have been used. And they must be completely dry before you use them again. So it is worth investing in several bags in various sizes, especially if you need to have two or three on the go at one time, with different nozzles, as you do when making the swans. I would suggest buying one large fabric bag, a couple of medium ones and a small one, so you can adapt to the quantity of batter you need to pipe. The bags have a small hole where the nozzle goes, and you can cut this to the correct size for the nozzle you want to use.

You can buy plastic nozzles, but I like the stainless steel ones, which give a sharper edge to the piping. Again, they come in different sizes, so I would have a set of plain nozzles in large, medium and small, and another set of star-shaped nozzles, again in large, medium and small.

To fill a piping bag cleanly, turn the bag inside out over one hand and use the other hand to fill it just half full. Pull up the sides of the bag and twist the top so that the mixture is forced down towards the nozzle.

As I explain on page 182, the way to pipe fluently and stay in control, is not to hold the bag in one hand and squeeze with the other, but to squeeze with the same hand that is holding the bag, with your other hand underneath, steadying and guiding as you pipe.

Keeping and freezing pastry

Salted, sweet and puff pastry will keep for up to a week in the fridge. However, I always make at least double the quantity of pastry I need and immediately freeze what I am not using. I wrap it first in greaseproof paper, then put it in a freezer bag and write the date on it. The pastry will keep for about three months in the freezer, and you will find that, after defrosting, it is a dream to roll out.

When pastry is going to be frozen for close to three months, it can discolour a little. If you don't want this to happen, add a drop of lemon juice or vinegar to the water before mixing it into the dough – you won't taste it in the pastry, but it will be enough to keep it fresh-looking.

If you like, you can roll out your pastry and line your tart tins, then freeze them, stacked inside one another, wrapped loosely in greaseproof paper inside a freezer bag. Simply defrost before use.

Alternatively, when using salted or sweet pastry, you can blind bake your pastry cases, remove them from their tins or rings and keep them in an airtight container for 2–3 days before filling.

In the Sweet chapter the tarts that contain almond cream can usually be frozen in their entirety, or at least up to the point of topping with fruit. Or they can be baked first, and then frozen – see page 119, together with the instructions in each recipe, for more details. You can also bake cheesecakes (see page 116 and picture opposite) in their entirety and then freeze them. When you defrost them, they are ready to eat. Just be aware that the pastry might not be quite as crispy as when it is freshly baked.

I don't recommend freezing choux pastry when it is raw, but once baked, you can put choux buns, éclairs and suchlike on a tray in the freezer, and when they are frozen, transfer them to a freezer container. Then you can defrost them and fill and/or glaze according to your recipe.

2   Salted

As I mentioned in the introduction, I call this chapter Salted, not because the pastry is full of salt, but because this was the generic name for savoury pastry that I learnt as an apprentice baker.

The recipes in this chapter are for all the kinds of things I associate with the traiteur in France, even though they include very British Cornish pasties, sausage rolls and pork pies. The traiteur's shop makes the best food to go, and the traiteur himself is like a multi-event athlete who has the skills of a baker, patissier, butcher, charcutier and chef without specialising in any one. When I was growing up, it was always a treat to go inside the shop and, from among the many dishes ready to take home, choose a slice of freshly made quiche, a wedge of pie or a small tart, with a selection of some of the big, colourful salads that would be set out in bowls.

Makes 24

1 quantity Salted Pastry (see page 16)

butter or baking spray, for greasing the tin(s)

1 egg, beaten with a pinch of salt, for sealing the pastry

For the base filling

400 g crème fraîche

4 large eggs

sea salt and freshly ground pepper

½ nutmeg, freshly grated

Savoury tarts

Yes, the dreaded quiche. In Britain it is so often associated with bland, soggy slices on the buffet table at parties, but in France it is a staple of the traiteur, and the quality of the pastry and the variety of fillings is a matter of pride. Personally, I think a freshly baked quiche, not long out of the oven, with a crisp salad dressed with good vinaigrette, is fantastic. In my classes, to help convert people, we start off by making small tartlets and individual ones rather than big quiches because it is so much easier to roll out the pastry and get it to crisp up well in the oven, eliminating the limp pastry factor that puts off so many people.

The base filling is a mixture of crème fraîche and eggs to which you can add any flavourings or ingredients you like. I use crème fraîche because it is light and has a slight tang, but if you prefer a richer, creamier texture, you can substitute it with double cream, or use half crème fraîche and half double cream. I have given three of my favourite fillings overleaf, but other ideas include chopped walnuts and Roquefort cheese, or even some slivers of roast chicken plus potatoes and vegetables left over from Sunday lunch. Varying the fillings helps keep the quiches interesting, and is a great idea for parties.

To make things simpler if you are catering for a number of people, you can blind bake the pastry cases up to two or three days in advance and keep them in an airtight container until you are ready to fill them and pop them in the oven for half an hour or so. I think the tartlets are at their best if you allow them to cool down to room temperature before eating: if they are too hot or too cold, the temperature suppresses the flavour.

I have chosen to make the quiches as tartlets, but they can be made bigger (26 cm) if you prefer (see page 16). However, you will need to double the quantity of your chosen filling, and bake them for about 30–35 minutes.

Make the pastry, then rest it in the fridge for at least 1 hour, preferably several, or, better still, overnight (see page 29).

Lightly grease two 12-hole tart tins. Skim a fine film of flour over your work surface, roll out the pastry 2–3 mm thick and use to line the tins (see pages 30–36). Line with baking paper and ceramic beans. Place in the fridge to rest for at least 30 minutes.

Preheat the oven to 190°C/Gas 5.

Remove the tins from the fridge and bake for 15 minutes. Lift out the paper and beans, brush the pastry with the beaten egg, then bake for another 8 minutes. Set aside (see pages 37–42).

Whisk the crème fraîche a little to loosen it, then mix in the eggs with a wooden spoon. (This is a tip I learnt from my days as an apprentice baker in France: using a spoon instead of a whisk prevents overmixing, which can make the filling dense. More restrained mixing helps to lift the filling so it becomes nice and light in the oven.) Season well and add the grated nutmeg.

Now you can flavour the base filling as you wish. The three combinations below are my favourites and each makes enough for 12 tartlets, but you can mix and match, and divide or multiply as you like.

Hot variations

Smoked salmon and parsley (or dill): Put 2 tomato halves and some salmon trimmings into each pastry case, with a little chopped parsley (or dill) on top. Spoon some of the base filling over the top and bake for 25–30 minutes.

Bacon, leek and reblochon: Gently heat a dry frying pan and, when hot, add 2 chopped slices

smoked bacon or 100 g smoked lardons. When golden, transfer to a sheet of kitchen paper to absorb the excess fat. Boil and slice 2 small potatoes and very finely slice the white part of 1 thin leek. Divide the bacon, potatoes and leek between the pastry cases. Spoon some of the base filling over the top and top with a slice of reblochon (or any cheese you like: Emmenthal, Port Salut, goats' cheese, Camembert, Brie or even Cheddar are fine). Bake for 25–30 minutes.

Mushroom and spinach: Melt a knob of butter in a frying pan, add 6 small quartered mushrooms and fry gently for a couple of minutes until they colour a little. Add 150 g baby spinach and cook quickly until it has wilted. Put the mixture into a sieve and drain off the excess liquid – there should be very little. Divide the mixture between the pastry cases. Spoon some of the base filling over the top and sprinkle with a little grated Gruyère. Bake for 25–30 minutes. (You could also use frozen spinach for this – just defrost it quickly and mix it with the sautéd mushrooms.)

Cold variations

If you like you can blind bake the tartlets and keep them in an airtight container until you are ready to fill them with ingredients that need no further cooking – a great idea for parties. Try fillings such as mayonnaise and poached salmon or trout, blanched green beans and a little dill (see picture opposite), smoked salmon and crème fraîche, smoked trout and creamed horseradish or smoked ham and chutney, or just experiment!

Makes 24

1 quantity Salted or Spelt Pastry (see page 16)

25 g butter

large pinch of sea salt

large pinch of sugar

6 onions, finely sliced

1 garlic clove, crushed

1 bay leaf

butter or baking spray, for greasing the tin(s)

1 tbsp Gruyère cheese, grated

24 small thyme sprigs

Onion tartlets

You don't need to blind bake the pastry for these tartlets as the filling isn't as liquid as the quiche filling on page 67. This means that you can make them up in their entirety and freeze them. Defrost them thoroughly, then bake as normal.

Make the pastry, then rest it in the fridge for at least 1 hour, preferably several, or, better still, overnight (see page 29).

Preheat the oven to 190°C/Gas 5.

Melt the butter in a heavy-based pan with the salt and sugar. Add the onions, garlic and bay leaf and cook slowly until the onions are softened and browned a little. Remove the bay leaf.

Lightly grease two 12-hole tart tins. Skim a fine film of flour over your work surface, roll out the pastry 2–3 mm thick and use to line the tins (see

pages 30–36). Place in the fridge to rest for at least 30 minutes.

Fill the chilled cases with the onion mixture, top with a little Gruyère and a sprig of thyme. Bake for 18–20 minutes, until the pastry cases and cheese are nicely browned.

Open tart

I sometimes like to make one large, rustic-looking tart, rather than the traditional round quiche. The hand-shaped tart is slid straight onto a preheated upturned grill pan or baking tray at a high heat, so there is no need to chill a lined tin or to blind bake the pastry; the heat of the tray will help to give a nice crisp base. In this case too, the topping is quite thin, so it will bake quickly.

Preheat the oven to 220°C/Gas 7 and, if necessary, put an upturned baking tray in to heat.

Roll one quantity of salted pastry (see page 16) into a rough circle, about 25 cm in diameter or an A4 rectangle about 5 mm thick. Place it on a sheet of baking parchment and use your fingers to pinch a high rim all the way around to contain the filling.

Use one of the savoury tartlet fillings on pages 68, and spoon it into the pastry case. Open the oven and carefully slide the tart, still on the baking paper, onto the hot grill pan or tray. Bake for 25 minutes until the pastry is golden.

Makes 1 large tart

1 quantity Semolina Pastry (see page 16)

butter or baking spray, for greasing the tin(s)

1 egg, beaten with a pinch of salt, for sealing the pastry

For the filling

100 g butter

100 g flour

1 litre milk, full fat or semi-skimmed

4 egg yolks

50 g Emmenthal cheese, grated

30 g Parmesan cheese, grated

2 tsp Dijon mustard

sea salt and freshly ground pepper

½ nutmeg, grated (or more, to taste)

500 g chicken meat, from breasts or thighs, or a mixture

2 tbsp light olive oil or rapeseed oil

250 g small button mushrooms

2 tbsp finely chopped tarragon

1 tbsp finely chopped parsley

Chicken & tarragon tarts

This tart has a really oozy, creamy filling, and makes a great contrast to the semolina pastry, which is a little shorter and crispier than the basic salted pastry, and has a slightly grainy texture.

Make the pastry, then rest it in the fridge for at least 1 hour, preferably several, or, better still, overnight (see page 29).

Preheat the oven to 190°C/Gas 5.

Lightly grease one 26 cm tart tin. Skim a fine film of flour over your work surface, roll out the pastry 5 mm thick and use to line the tin (see pages 30–36). Line with baking paper and ceramic beans. Put into the fridge to rest for 30 minutes. Remove the tin from the fridge, place on a baking tray and bake for 20 minutes. Lift out the paper and beans, brush the pastry with the beaten egg, then bake for another 10 minutes. Set aside (see pages 37–41).

Lower the oven to 180°C/Gas 4.

To make the filling, melt the butter in a pan, add the flour and cook for 1 minute, whisking all the time. Add the milk gradually, whisking continuously until the mixture comes to the boil. Lower the heat to a simmer and let the mixture

cook, continuing to whisk, for at least 1 more minute, until it thickens. Whisk in the egg yolks, cheeses and mustard, then taste and season with salt, pepper and nutmeg. Take off the heat and leave to cool.

Cut the chicken into fine strips. Heat the oil in a frying pan and gently cook the chicken for around 4–5 minutes – it needs to be cooked through, so break a piece open to check. Remove the chicken, drain on kitchen paper and set aside.

Add the mushrooms to the frying pan and brown them a little (just for a minute or two). Add them to the filling, along with the reserved chicken and herbs, and stir well. Spoon into the pastry case.

Put back onto the baking tray and bake for 20–25 minutes, until the filling is golden and just set if you wobble the tray. You can either eat the tart warm and runny (I love it like this), or put it in the fridge to set and eat cold with a big green salad.

Makes 8 x 10 cm tarts

1 quantity Spelt Pastry (see page 16)

butter or baking spray, for greasing the tins

1 egg, beaten with a pinch of salt, for sealing the pastry

For the filling

2 butternut squash

3 tbsp olive oil

3 eggs

250 g ricotta cheese

80 g Parmesan cheese, grated

1 tbsp chopped sage leaves

sea salt and freshly ground pepper

Pumpkin & ricotta tarts

If you like, you can blind-bake the pastry cases two or three days in advance and keep them in an airtight container until you are ready to fill and bake them.

Don't throw away the squash seeds, as you can toast them and then use them to decorate the tarts, or eat as a snack, sprinkled with sea salt. Just spread them out on a baking tray and put them in the oven for the last 8–10 minutes of the roasting time for the squash, until they are lightly toasted.

Make the pastry then rest it in the fridge for at least 1 hour, preferably several, or, better still, overnight (see page 29).

Preheat the oven to 200ºC/Gas 6.

Cut the butternut squash lengthways into quarters. Remove the seeds, but don't throw away them away (see above). Place the quartered squash in a baking tray and drizzle with the olive oil. Roast in the oven for 40–45 minutes, or until the flesh is soft.

Lower the heat to 190ºC/Gas 5. Lightly grease eight 10 cm loose-bottomed tins, about 2 cm deep.

Skim a fine film of flour over your work surface, roll out the pastry 2–3 mm thick and use to line the tins (see pages 30–34). Line with baking paper and ceramic beans. Place in the fridge to rest for at least 30 minutes.

Remove the tins from the fridge, place on baking trays and bake for 15 minutes. Lift out the paper and beans, brush the pastry with the beaten egg, then bake for another 8 minutes. Set aside (see pages 37–41).

Lower the heat to 180ºC/Gas 4.

Mix the eggs and ricotta together in a bowl. Stir in the Parmesan and sage.

When the butternut squash is cool enough to handle, scrape the flesh from the skin into a bowl and mash it with a masher or fork. Stir it into the cheese mixture and season. Spoon the mixture into the pastry cases, put back onto the baking trays and bake in the oven for 20 minutes, until the filling is just set and golden brown. Remove and eat warm, or allow to cool and put in the fridge to eat cold.

Makes 4 large pasties (about 16 cm long), or 10 small pasties (about 10 cm long)

1 quantity Salted Pastry, made with margarine, not butter (see page 16)

butter or baking spray, for greasing the baking tray

1 egg, beaten with a pinch of salt, for glazing the pastry

For the filling

1 medium swede

1 large potato

1 large onion

400 g good-quality skirt or chuck steak, diced quite small

sea salt and freshly ground pepper

Cornish pasties

Originally, the pasty was poor man's food, made for Cornish field workers and miners to take to work with them. As a Breton, I know I am walking into a minefield here because there is so much controversy about what makes an authentic pasty. Although most recipes would have lard in the pastry, I prefer to use my usual salted pastry, though made with block margarine instead of butter to keep it feeling authentic and give the traditional flaky softness required.

Purists, I know, insist that the filling should be made with turnip, not swede, and that the pasty should be crimped around the side, not over the top. But this is *my* version, and I like crimping over the top because it looks more distinctive and less like an apple turnover.

You can make up the pasties completely, brush them with beaten egg and then freeze them. Before baking, defrost them completely (allow 3–4 hours, and insert a skewer into the centre to check that they are defrosted all the way through), then bake as normal.

Make the pastry, then rest it in the fridge for at least 1 hour, preferably several, or, better still, overnight (see page 29).

Preheat the oven to 210°C/Gas 7.

Roll out the pastry 2–3 mm thick (for small pasties) or 5 mm (for large ones) and cut out circles either 16 cm or 10 cm in diameter. (Use a pastry cutter or cut around a plate.) Stack up the circles, interleaving them with greaseproof paper, and put in the fridge while you make the filling.

Peel the swede, potato and onion, and cut into small cubes around 1.5 cm – don't worry about perfection, but try to keep them roughly the same size so they will cook evenly. Put all the vegetables in a bowl with the diced steak, mix together and season well, especially with black pepper.

Divide the filling between the chilled pastry circles, spooning it into the centre of each circle. Brush a little water around the edge of the pastry, then bring the sides together and crimp neatly over the top.

Place the pasties on a lightly greased baking tray and brush them with beaten egg. With the tip of a sharp knife, make a small hole just to one side of the crimping to allow steam to escape. Bake for 10 minutes, then lower the heat to 180°C/Gas 4 and bake for another 30 minutes, until golden brown and the base is brown and firm.

Serves 12

1 quantity Caraway Pastry (see page 16)

butter or baking spray, for greasing the tin

flour, for dusting

For the filling

200 g pork belly

200 g pork shoulder

200 g duck leg meat

200 g duck liver, diced

6 juniper berries

2 tsp whole allspice

1 tsp whole green peppercorns

1 tsp sweet smoked paprika

1 large thyme sprig, leaves only

200 ml sherry or port

18 small shallots, unpeeled

light olive oil or rapeseed oil

1 smoked duck breast

2 large eggs

150 ml single cream

sea salt and freshly ground pepper

For the jelly

3 gelatine leaves

200 ml good chicken stock

100 ml sweet sherry or port

For the topping

3 medium golden (or striped) beetroot

3 red beetroot

a few sprigs of rosemary and thyme

olive oil

Duck pie

This is a fantastic, rich, open pie that is finished with a little sherry or port jelly poured into it after baking. It is served cold, topped with roasted beetroot and shallots, so it looks quite spectacular. You can find beetroot in all sorts of colours and stripes in good greengrocers or farm shops, so have fun with the topping. I promise it is much simpler to make than it sounds; you just need to allow plenty of time. Ideally, start the night before: make the pastry and line the tin, then put the meat in a bowl to marinate, and keep both in the fridge overnight. If you're pushed for time, a couple of hours in the fridge for both is fine, but note that once you have made the pie, cooled it for 2 hours, then poured in the jelly, it will need to go back into the fridge to set for another 4–5 hours. For deep game and pork pies like this I always dust the greased tin with flour, which seems to help the finish of the pastry.

Make the pastry then rest it in the fridge for at least 1 hour, preferably several, or, better still, overnight (see page 29).

Trim and dice the pork belly and shoulder, duck legs and liver and place in a bowl. Add the spices, thyme and sherry, stir, then leave to marinate for at least 2–3 hours, but preferably overnight, in the fridge. Give the bowl a shake from time to time.

Lightly grease a 20 cm loose-bottomed square or round cake tin and tip in a little flour. Tilt the tin around so that every surface is lightly dusted, then tip out the excess.

Remove the pastry from the fridge and roll it out on a very lightly floured surface (see page 30) to form a square or circle about 5 mm thick and twice the size of your tin (i.e. 40 cm square or in diameter).

Lift the pastry over the tin and gently line it (see page 33). Place it back into the fridge for at least 30 minutes, or until the meat has finished marinating.

When you are ready to make the pie, preheat the oven to 180°C/Gas 4.

Put the unpeeled shallots in a pan with enough light olive oil or rapeseed oil to cover and simmer very slowly for 10–15 minutes, until they are soft and can be easily pierced with the tip of a knife. Leave to cool, then slice off the base and squeeze from the other end so that the shallots pop out of their skins. Keep the shallot flesh to one side.

Dice the smoked duck breast, then set aside.

Remove the marinated meat from the fridge and put through a mincer (use the largest hole), or chop finely with a large knife.

Mix the eggs and cream together in a bowl, stir in the minced meat, add the diced duck breast and season. To test that it is seasoned to your liking, take a little bit of the mixture and fry it in a pan. Make sure it is cooked through, then taste it and adjust if necessary. Now mix in half of the shallots.

Take your pastry case out of the fridge and fill it with the meat mixture.

Cover the top with a piece of greaseproof paper to stop the pastry browning too quickly, place on a baking tray and bake for 1½–1¾ hours, or until the meat is cooked through. During the baking, rotate the pie and move it around the oven if necessary so that the pastry is evenly baked. You can test this by inserting a metal skewer into some pieces of meat and checking that the skewer comes out piping hot. For the last 30 minutes remove the greaseproof paper.

Take the pie from the oven and leave to cool for at least 2 hours.

To make the jelly, soak the gelatine leaves briefly in cold water, just long enough to soften them. Squeeze out the excess water.

Heat the chicken stock and sherry in a pan, then add the squeezed gelatine. Stir well until the gelatine has dissolved. Take off the heat and leave to cool a little, but not too much or the jelly will start to get too thick to pour.

Now take the cold pie (still in its tin). You will notice that the meat has separated a little from the pastry case so pour the sherry jelly into the gap and over the top of the meat. Put the pie in the fridge so that the jelly sets. This will take 4–5 hours, but the pie will be at its best after 24 hours (it will keep in the fridge for up to a week if you don't want to eat it straight away).

Before serving, heat the oven again to 200°C/Gas 6.

Wash the unpeeled beetroot and put them whole into a pan of water. Bring to the boil, then lower the heat and simmer for about 20 minutes, until you can slide the tip of a knife into the beetroot, but there is still a bit of resistance. Lift out and, when cool enough to handle, cut into wedges, leaving the peel on and any little bits of root or stalk – these give the wedges character and will make the topping for your pie look even more eye-catching. Place in a baking tin with the rosemary and thyme, drizzle with a little olive oil, and roast in the oven for about 25 minutes, or until tender. Remove and allow to cool.

When the jelly has set, ease the whole pie carefully from the tin, arrange the beetroot wedges and reserved shallots on top, and serve.

Makes 8

butter or lard, for greasing the moulds

flour, for dusting the moulds and rolling

1 egg, beaten with a pinch of salt, for glazing the pastry

For the hot-water crust

1 egg

450 g plain flour

175 g lard (or goose or duck fat)

5 g (1 tsp) salt

5 g (1 tsp) sugar

For the filling

300 g pork belly, skin removed

300 g pork shoulder

2 anchovies in oil, drained

2 tbsp chopped fresh sage leaves

200 g smoked bacon or pancetta

½ nutmeg seed, freshly grated

sea salt and freshly ground pepper

For the jelly

3 gelatine leaves

200 ml good chicken stock

100 ml sweet sherry or port

Pork pies

Consider this a bonus recipe that stands apart from the others in this chapter because it uses hot-water crust, which is a different type of pastry from those described previously. It is used only for making raised pies that are eaten cold.

Raised pies are something that the British have always been good at making, from the humble to the elaborate, filled with all kinds of meat, game and fruit, but the one I loved instantly when I came to England was the individual, pure pork pie. Well-seasoned and made properly with good-quality meat and great jelly, it is just beautiful.

Traditionally, the jelly is made using a pig's trotter, and there is a recipe for this on page 98, but if you are short of time you can make the simple version on page 96, which I also use for the Duck Pie on page 81. In most traditional recipes the pastry is also hand-raised, which means that it is shaped without the help of a mould. However, I know that many people find the idea of doing this quite daunting, so these pies are made in a much easier way, in dariole moulds.

If you don't want to try the hot-water crust, you could make these pies using Cornish pasty pastry (see page 16). It will obviously have a slightly different flavour and texture, but you will still have some very tasty pies!

First make the pastry. Break your egg into a small bowl. Put the flour into a large bowl and make a well in the centre. Add the egg to the flour and stir in briefly.

Put the lard in a pan with 175 ml water, the salt and sugar. Bring to the boil, stirring as the lard melts. When it comes to the boil, count to 30 seconds and immediately take the pan off the heat. Pour the liquid into the flour mixture, stirring continuously with a wooden spoon

When the mixture forms quite a sticky dough, cover the bowl with a clean tea towel and leave to rest and cool for 1 hour.

Turn the dough onto a lightly floured work surface (see page 24). Flatten it out with your hands.

Fold the dough into thirds by taking one side into the centre and pressing down with your fingertips.

Next, bring the opposite side over the top.

Press down again with your fingertips.

Flatten the dough into a rough oblong shape, lift onto a baking tray, then cover with greaseproof paper and put into the fridge to rest for at least 30 minutes.

Preheat the oven to 180°C/Gas 4.

While the pastry is resting, make the filling. Dice the pork belly and shoulder roughly and mix with the anchovies and sage. Put this mixture into a food mixer with a mincer attachment (use the one with the larger holes) and grind to the texture of mincemeat. Alternatively, place in a food processor and pulse briefly, stopping and starting, until you have the required texture. (By pulsing in short bursts you will avoid overdoing it and ending up with meat paste.) If you don't have a machine, you can chop all the meat very finely with a big knife; it is just a bit more tedious.

Cut the bacon or pancetta into small pieces and stir into the minced meat. Add the nutmeg, then season and mix well. To test that it is seasoned to your liking, take a little bit of the mixture and fry it in a pan. Make sure it is cooked through, then taste it and adjust if necessary.

Take the pastry out of the fridge – by now it should be firmer. Roll it briefly on a lightly floured work surface (see page 30). Fold it into three and roll out again about 3–4 mm thick.

Finally, using a pastry cutter or saucer about 12 cm in diameter, cut out eight circles. Now use a cutter or glass tumbler 8 cm in diameter to cut out another eight.

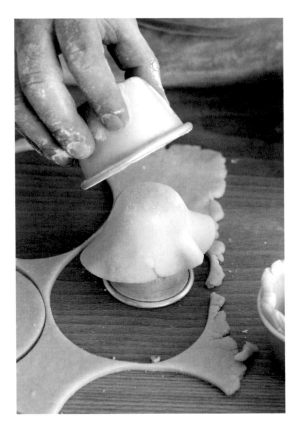 

Lightly grease 8 dariole moulds, then dust with flour, emptying out the excess. Line each mould with a circle of pastry, pushing it gently into the base and against the sides, and leaving about 1 cm overhanging the rim. An easy way of doing this is to drape your pastry over a smaller upturned mould or glass, then put the dariole mould you want to line over the top.

Turn both over and remove the smaller mould or glass.

With your fingertips, press the pastry well into the base and sides of the mould.

Repeat with the rest of the moulds. Now you are ready to fill them.

Divide the meat mixture between them, then tap each mould on the work surface to help the meat settle down. Put an 8 cm circle of pastry over the top of each mould. Starting in the centre and working outwards to the edges, press it gently onto the meat with your fingertips without stretching it.

Crimp the edges of the pastry together all around, making sure they are firmly sealed.

Brush the top of each pie with the beaten egg, then use a skewer to make a hole in the top of each one to allow steam to escape in the oven.

Place the moulds on a baking tray and bake for 40 minutes, or until the meat is cooked through (a skewer inserted into the centre of the pies should come out piping hot, or a meat probe should register 87–90°C). Leave the pies to cool for at least 2 hours.

Meanwhile, make the jelly. Soak the gelatine leaves in cold water for at least a couple of minutes to soften them, then squeeze out the excess water.

Heat the chicken stock and sherry in a pan, then add the squeezed gelatine. Stir well until the

gelatine has dissolved. Take off the heat and leave to cool a little, but not too much or the jelly will start to get too thick to pour.

When the pies are cool, take a little funnel, piping nozzle or a syringe (or make a small cone with some greaseproof paper) and push it into the hole you made in each pie. Carefully pour or syringe in enough jelly to come to the top. Put in the fridge for 8 hours to set, then turn out and eat!

1 pig's trotter or 1 chicken carcass

3 gelatine leaves (only if using a chicken carcass)

1 bay leaf

1 carrot

1 onion

6 peppercorns

Traditional pork pie jelly

When you make this with a pig's trotter it is naturally gelatinous and needs no additional thickening, but if you make it with a chicken carcass, you will need to add some leaf gelatine, as indicated below. This recipe makes a generous amount, and you will need only 300 ml of it for the Pork Pie recipe on page 85, so freeze any left over for another occasion.

Place the pig's trotter or chicken carcass and all the other ingredients in a saucepan with 2 litres water and bring to the boil. Skim the scum from the surface, then lower the heat and simmer for 2 hours, skimming regularly. Take off the heat and pour the liquid through a sieve into clean pan. Bring to the boil and simmer for 10 more minutes to reduce and thicken a little more.

If you have used a chicken carcass rather than a pig's trotter, soak the gelatine in cold water for a few minutes to soften, then squeeze dry. Place in a small bowl, then add a little of the hot liquid and stir to dissolve. Add this to the pan and stir until the liquid has thickened.

Take the pan from the heat, leave to cool, then use to fill the pork pies (see page 96).

Makes about 20

1 quantity Salted Pastry (see page 16), but substitute all the plain flour with wholemeal spelt flour

1 tbsp wholegrain spelt

Spelt biscuits

These crispy wafer biscuits, which are great with cheese, are made with spelt pastry, a variation of salted. I substitute all the flour in the basic recipe with wholemeal spelt flour and add some extra wholegrain spelt so that you get a really good, crunchy texture.

Make the pastry as usual (see page 16), but add the wholegrain spelt to the spelt flour at the beginning. Rest the neatly squared-off pastry in the fridge for at least 1 hour, preferably several, or, better still, overnight (see page 29). The firmer it is the better.

Preheat the oven to 160°C/Gas 3.

Using a very sharp knife, cut the chilled pastry into wafers about 2–3 mm thick. Lay these on one or more baking trays and bake for 10–12 minutes. They will be a dark golden colour, thanks to the spelt. Remove from the oven and leave to cool and crisp up a little on the tray(s) before transferring to a rack to cool completely. The biscuits will keep in an airtight container for 2–3 weeks.

3   Sweet

My earliest memories of sweet pastries are of Sundays mornings in Brittany when, like most families, we would go to the boulangerie/ patisserie and choose a selection to have after Sunday lunch: perhaps some apple or apricot tarts, or pear *bourdaloue*, with its frangipane puffed up and golden around the fruit. There might be some choux pastry swans with ruffled chantilly cream 'feathers', and in summer always fresh strawberry tarts, with the fruit glistening on a layer of beautiful vanilla crème patissière. During the week you might make a simple fruit tart at home, but on Sundays the tradition is still to treat the family to something special, beautifully presented in a box tied with ribbon.

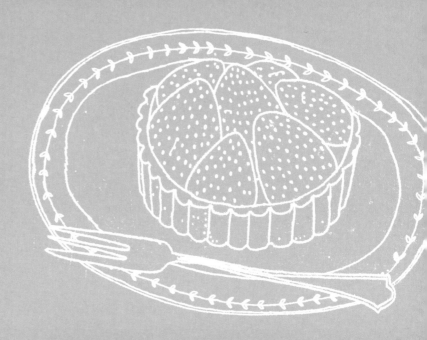

In Britain there is much more enthusiasm for baking at home any day of the week, and I don't think you can beat a classic sweet tart at any time of the day: with a coffee in the morning, a cup of tea in the afternoon, or as a dessert after dinner. The key is to keep the pastry thin enough in proportion to the topping so that it has an elegant crispness to it.

Most of the tarts that follow can be eaten warm or cold, though by cold I mean at room temperature. So often we have a tendency to eat things when they are piping hot or straight from the fridge, and at either extreme the temperature dulls the flavour. Even if you keep a refreshing, fresh fruit tart in the fridge, it will taste just a little bit more special if you allow it to come up to room temperature before serving it.

Makes 24 x 8 cm tarts

1 quantity Sweet Pastry (see page 17)

butter or baking spray, for greasing the tins

1 egg, beaten with a pinch of salt, for sealing the pastry

dash of kirsch (if using strawberries) or rum (optional)

For the crème patissière

250 ml full-fat milk (semi-skimmed could be used if you prefer, but the cream will not be as rich)

1 vanilla pod

3 egg yolks

60 g caster sugar

25 g plain flour

For the topping

about 750 g strawberries or any other fresh fruit

about 200 g clear apricot jam, to glaze, or icing sugar, to dust

mint leaves (optional), for decoration

Fruit tartlets

These are classic tarts made with fresh fruits on a creamy base. Crème patissière – literally pastry chef's cream – is often confused with crème anglaise, which is the French name for custard. They are very similar, but whereas custard is set only with eggs, crème patissière also uses flour (or cornflour) so that it is thicker and can be used as a base or filling for all kinds of pastries. It is at the heart of the pastry-maker's craft and you will find it used frequently in the puff pastry chapter as well as here.

I prefer to make my crème patissière in the more traditional way, with flour rather than cornflour. Cornflour gives more of a sheen, but I feel I can taste it in the finished cream.

The key to making good crème patissière is in the final stage. Once the hot milk has been whisked into the eggs, flour and sugar, it goes back onto the heat, and – this is the important bit – it needs to come to the boil and then keep boiling for a minute while you whisk continuously. This is what cooks the mixture so that you don't taste any flouriness in the finished cream, and makes it set properly.

I like to teach people how to make these tarts in my pastry classes, not only because they involve the all-important crème patissière, but because once you master making impressive-looking small tartlets, it is easy to move on to bigger ones and feel confident about it.

This recipe makes enough for 24 tartlets made in 8 cm tins. Of course I know most people aren't going to have that many tins, but you can bake them blind in batches 2–3 days in advance if you like, and keep them in an airtight container ready to fill with the pastry cream and top with fruit when you want to serve them. Or, if you want to make a smaller batch, you can freeze whatever pastry you don't need for another time (see page 63).

The tarts can be made to look very smart by cutting and arranging the various fruits in the way professional pastry chefs do it (see page 200–204).

Make the pastry, then rest it in the fridge for at least 1 hour, preferably several, or, better still, overnight (see page 29).

To make the crème patissière, put the milk into a heavy-based saucepan. Using a sharp knife, split the vanilla pod along its length, scrape the seeds into the milk, then put the halved pods in too.

Put the egg yolks and sugar into a bowl and whisk until pale and creamy. Add the flour and mix until smooth.

Put the pan of milk over a medium heat, bring to just under the boil, then slowly pour half of it into the egg mixture, whisking well as you do so. Add the remainder of the milk and whisk again, then pour the mixture back into the pan. Bring to the boil, whisking all the time, then keep boiling and whisking continuously for 1 minute. Take off the heat.

Pour the mixture into a clean bowl and scoop out the vanilla pods. (You can wash and dry them and keep them in a jar of sugar, which will give you vanilla-flavoured sugar for use in all your baking.) Cover the surface of the bowl with greaseproof paper straight away to prevent a skin forming. Allow to cool, then store in the fridge until you're ready to use it.

Lightly grease 24 loose-bottomed tins, 8 cm in diameter and 2 cm deep. (If you don't have this many tins, you can bake in batches.)

Skim a fine film of flour over your work surface, roll out the pastry 2–3 mm thick and use to line the tins (see pages 30–34). Line with baking paper and ceramic beans. Place in the fridge to rest for at least 30 minutes.

Preheat the oven to 190°C/Gas 5.

Remove the tins from the fridge, place on a baking tray and bake for 15 minutes. Lift out the paper and beans, brush the pastry with the beaten egg, then bake for another 8 minutes. Set aside (see pages 37–41). Leave in the tins for about 15 minutes, then lift out and leave on a rack until cold.

Fill the pastry cases with crème patissière (mixed with a little kirsch, if you like, if using strawberries) and top with your fresh fruit.

To glaze the tarts, put the jam into a pan with a tablespoon or two of water, and bring to just under a simmer – don't let it boil or the jam will become too gooey to spread properly. Using a pastry brush, lightly glaze the top of each tart. Alternatively, dust the tartlets with icing sugar.

Decorate, if you like, with mint leaves.

Makes 24 x 8 cm tartlets

1 quantity Sweet Pastry (see page 17)

butter or baking spray, for greasing the tins

1 egg, beaten with a pinch of salt, for sealing the pastry

icing sugar, for glazing (optional)

For the filling

7 unwaxed lemons

9 eggs

400 g caster sugar

250 g double cream

Lemon tarts

I like to make small lemon tartlets, but you can make them in other sizes if you wish (see page 17); you might prefer just a big one (26 x 4 cm), which can be cut into slices. You can blind bake the pastry cases in batches, 2–3 days in advance if you like, and keep them in an airtight container, ready to fill. You can then finish the baking when you want to serve them.

If you have any lemon filling left over, it needn't be wasted: spoon it into ramekins and bake in the same way, but without the pastry. Served with biscuits and a little crème fraîche, it makes a lovely pudding.

Make the pastry, then rest it in the fridge for at least 1 hour, preferably several, or, better still, overnight (see page 29).

Lightly grease 24 loose-bottomed tins, 8 cm in diameter and 2 cm deep. (If you don't have this many tins, you can bake in batches.)

Skim a fine film of flour over your work surface, roll out the pastry 2–3 mm thick and use to line the tins (see pages 30–34). Line with baking paper and ceramic beans. Place in the fridge to rest for at least 30 minutes.

Preheat the oven to 190ºC/Gas 5.

Remove the tins from the fridge, place on a baking tray and bake for 15 minutes. Lift out the paper and beans, brush the pastry with the beaten egg, then bake for another 8 minutes. Set aside (see pages 37–41).

Lower the oven to 150ºC/Gas 2.

To make the filling, zest four of the lemons and squeeze the juice from all of them. Whisk the eggs, sugar and lemon zest in a large bowl until smooth, then add the lemon juice. Lightly whip the cream and fold it into the egg mixture. Skim any froth from the top, then pour into the pastry cases.

Bake for about 15 minutes, until the filling doesn't wobble if you shake the tins very gently, and the centre feels just set when touched. Don't wait until it feels very firm, as it will firm up a little as it cools.

Leave in the tins for about 15 minutes, then lift out and cool on a rack for 2 hours before eating. If you like, before serving, you can dust the top of each tart with a little icing sugar and melt with a blowtorch to glaze.

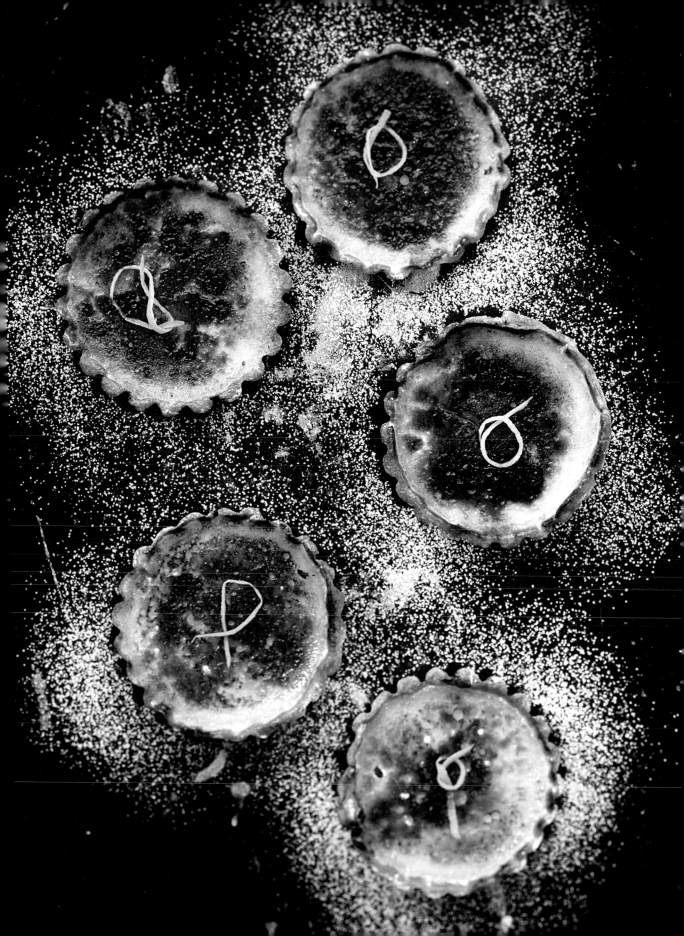

Makes 1 large tart approx. 35 x 11 cm

1 quantity Chocolate Pastry (see page 17)

about 12 fresh cherries, stalks still attached, or 24 cherries in alcohol or syrup, or 24 frozen cherries, defrosted

100 ml kirsch, if using tinned or frozen cherries

butter or baking spray, for greasing the tin

1 egg, beaten with a pinch of salt, for sealing the pastry

50 g cocoa powder, for dusting

For the chocolate fondant

140 g sugar

4 eggs

4 egg yolks

320 g good-quality dark chocolate (at least 70% cocoa solids)

320 g unsalted butter

100 g plain flour

Chocolate cherry tart

This is a beautiful tart to make when fresh cherries are in season. I like it best when it is still a little warm and the chocolate is quite soft and gooey, like a good chocolate brownie, but if you like a firmer texture, you can leave it to cool completely. Either way, it's gorgeous with cream. I think it is fun to leave the stalks on the cherries so that they pop out of the tart.

If you want to make this tart out of season, you can still do it using cherries preserved in alcohol or syrup. Failing that, you could use frozen or tinned cherries, and in both cases soak them in kirsch before use. However, you will need more preserved cherries than if using fresh because they are less plump and will disappear more into the chocolate fondant.

I like to make the tart rectangular and cut it into squares to serve, but you can make it circular or any shape you wish.

Make the pastry, then rest it in the fridge for at least 1 hour, preferably several, or, better still, overnight (see page 29).

If using tinned or defrosted cherries, drain them and put them into a bowl with the kirsch. Leave to soak overnight.

Lightly grease a loose-bottomed tart tin, approximately 35 x 11 cm and 2 cm deep.

Skim a fine film of flour over your work surface, roll out the pastry 5 mm thick and use to line the tin (see pages 30–34). Line with baking paper and ceramic beans. Place in the fridge to rest for at least 30 minutes.

Meanwhile, make the chocolate fondant. In a mixing bowl whisk the sugar, eggs and egg yolks until they are pale and have a creamy, mousse-like consistency.

Break the chocolate into chunks and put into a heatproof bowl. Place this over a pan of simmering water – you need enough water to come close to the bottom of the bowl but not actually touch it. Turn the heat very low so that you don't get steam into the bowl, as this can make the chocolate stiffen and look dull. Let the chocolate melt slowly, stirring all the time, then add the butter and keep stirring until it has melted. Take off the heat and add to the sugar and egg mixture, again stirring well until it is all incorporated. Gently fold in the flour and keep to one side.

Preheat the oven to 190ºC/Gas 5.

Remove the tin from the fridge, place on a baking tray and bake for 20 minutes. Lift out the paper and beans, brush the pastry with the beaten egg, then bake for another 10 minutes. Set aside (see pages 37–41).

Lower the oven to 180ºC/Gas 4.

Spread the fondant over the cooled pastry up to the top, then push the cherries into it, leaving some of the fruit showing (if using fresh cherries, leave the stalks sticking out). Put back on the baking tray and return to the oven for 12 minutes, until just set. The fondant will have risen a little, but, like a chocolate brownie, it should be only just firm to the touch as it will set a bit more when it cools. Leave in the tin for about 15 minutes, then lift out and cool on a rack.

The tart can be served either warm and gooey, or completely cold, when the chocolate will be a bit firmer. Dust with cocoa powder before serving.

Variation

Use sliced ripe (or tinned) pears instead of cherries.

Makes 24 x 8 cm tarts

1 quantity Sweet or Lemon Pastry (see page 17)

butter or baking spray, for greasing the tins

1 egg, beaten with a pinch of salt, for sealing the pastry

For the lemon curd filling

juice and zest of 3 unwaxed lemons

3 large eggs

200 g caster sugar

125 g unsalted butter

1 tsp cornflour

For the meringue

6 egg whites

360 g sugar

Lemon meringue tartlets

These tartlets are filled with lemon curd, but you could use the lemon filling from the recipe on page 108 if you like. Of course you can make a bigger tart (see page 17), but I think small tartlets are more fun because you can be a bit wild with the meringue. You can blind bake the pastry cases in batches, 2–3 days in advance, and keep them in an airtight container, ready to fill. You can then finish the baking when you want to serve them.

Make the pastry, then rest it in the fridge for at least 1 hour, preferably several, or, better still, overnight (see page 29).

To make the lemon curd, whisk all the ingredients together in a bowl, then place over a pan of simmering water. Make sure the water doesn't actually touch the base of the bowl. Heat very gently, whisking all the time, making sure you move the mixture around so it doesn't stick to the sides. Be patient, otherwise you will end up with scrambled eggs (if this should happen, put the mixture through a fine sieve very quickly, then back onto the heat). When it starts to look a little thicker than double cream, cook for 1 minute more and it should be ready. To test, blob a little of the mixture onto the inside of the bowl towards the top. It should stay still without dripping. Set aside to cool.

Lightly grease 24 loose-bottomed tins, 8 cm in diameter and 2 cm deep. (If you don't have this many tins, you can bake in batches.)

Skim a fine film of flour over your work surface, roll out the pastry 2–3 mm thick and use to line the tins (see pages 30–34). Line with baking paper and ceramic beans. Place in the fridge to rest for at least 30 minutes.

Preheat the oven to 190ºC/Gas 5.

Remove the tins from the fridge, place on baking trays and bake for 15 minutes. Lift out the paper and beans, brush the pastry with the beaten egg, put back on the baking trays then bake for another 8 minutes. Set aside (see pages 37–41).

Half-fill each pastry case with the lemon curd and put into the fridge until set.

Meanwhile, make the meringue. Whisk the egg whites until they form soft peaks. Put the sugar into a pan with 80 ml water and bring to the boil over a medium heat. At first you will see large bubbles; after 5–8 minutes, when some of the water has evaporated, the bubbles will be smaller. At this point you will have a thin, colourless syrup (if you have a sugar thermometer it will register 121ºC).

Wrap a tea towel around the bowl of egg whites and wedge it into a saucepan or larger bowl on your work surface so that it is held steady. Using one hand, pour in the syrup in a steady stream while whisking with the other hand, until the mixture becomes shiny and forms proper peaks. (Alternatively, you can whisk the egg whites in a food mixer fitted with a whisk attachment, and add the syrup with the motor turning.)

Fit a piping bag with a star nozzle (see page 61) and fill with the meringue. Take the pastry cases from the fridge and pipe the meringue over the lemon curd, going round and round and upwards to create peaks that are as wild as you like (see picture).

As the egg in the meringue has already been cooked by the hot syrup, the tarts need no further baking, but I think the meringue looks smarter and has more definition if the tips are lightly browned. The best way to do this is with a blowtorch, as it allows you to control which areas of the meringue you colour. The browning could also be done under a medium grill or in a hot oven (200ºC/Gas 6), but watch carefully to make sure the meringue doesn't caramelise and burn.

Makes 8 x 10 cm cheesecakes

1 quantity Sweet Pastry (see page 17)

butter or baking spray, for greasing the tins

1 egg, beaten with a pinch of salt, for sealing the pastry

For the filling

450 g cream cheese

200 g caster sugar

seeds from 1 large vanilla pod, or 1 tsp vanilla extract

4 whole eggs

2 egg yolks

400 g mascarpone

2 tsp plain flour

Mascarpone cheesecake

I wasn't a huge fan of cheesecake until I tasted the one made by Ronnie Bonetti at Babington House. Inspired by his original recipe I came up with the variations below. Of course you can make one big cheesecake if you prefer (see picture on page 63).

Make the pastry, then rest it in the fridge for at least 1 hour, preferably several, or, better still, overnight (see page 29).

Lightly grease eight 10 x 2 cm loose-bottomed tins.

Skim a fine film of flour over your work surface, roll out the pastry 2–3 mm thick and use to line the tins (see pages 30–34). Line with baking paper and ceramic beans. Place in the fridge to rest for at least 30 minutes.

Preheat the oven to 190ºC/Gas 5.

Remove the tins from the fridge, place on baking trays and bake for 15 minutes. Lift out the paper and beans, brush the pastry with the beaten egg, then bake for another 8 minutes. Set aside (see pages 37–41). Lower the oven to 150ºC/Gas 2.

To make the filling, put the cream cheese, sugar and vanilla into a bowl and beat until smooth. Beat in the eggs and yolks, then add the mascarpone, stirring until just incorporated. Fold in the flour. Divide the filling between each of the tart cases,

put back on the baking trays and bake for 45 minutes, until just set. Leave in the tins for about 15 minutes, then lift out and cool on a rack.

Variations

Passion fruit cheesecakes: Take 4 or 5 ripe passion fruit, cut in half and scrape the pulp into a small pan. Warm gently without boiling. Stir into the mascarpone mixture after you have folded in the flour.

Lemon cheesecakes: Omit the vanilla seeds and mix the juice and zest of 2 unwaxed lemons with the eggs and egg yolks before adding them to the cream cheese mixture.

Blackcurrant (or other red fruit) cheesecakes: Put 250 g ripe fruit in a small pan, crush slightly with a fork and warm gently, just to release the juices. Fill the pastry cases with the mascarpone mixture, then pour the fruit and juices over each one, swirling the top with a small knife.

Makes 4 x 16 cm tarts

1 quantity Sweet or Almond Pastry (see page 17)

butter or baking spray, for greasing the tins

2 tbsp flaked almonds

icing sugar, for dusting, or apricot glaze (see pages 105–106)

For the almond cream

250 g unsalted butter

250 g caster sugar

250 g ground almonds

50 g flour

3 eggs

2 tbsp Poire William liqueur or rum, or equivalent

Amandine

....

This is the classic almond tart made with *crème d'amande* (almond cream, also known as frangipane) and topped with flaked almonds. It is very like Bakewell tart, but without the layer of jam that goes in before the almond cream, and the name sounds more chic! A slice with coffee is just brilliant. The almond cream also forms the basis of many of the fruit tarts that follow. I even use it is a topping for my Mince Pies (see page 136). While you can mix the cream by hand, it is easier to get it light and fluffy with a mixer.

One of the great things about making tarts with almond cream is that they freeze well, so virtually any in which it is used can be fully baked and then frozen. When needed, simply defrost (allow 1–2 hours), then put into a preheated oven at 180°C/Gas 4 for about 6 minutes to freshen them up and recrisp the pastry a little.

Alternatively you can make up the tarts completely, ready to bake, and *then* freeze them. Just place them on a baking tray, loosely covered with an opened-out freezer bag, and freeze until hard, then stack them between layers of greaseproof paper in a plastic freezer box. They can then be baked without defrosting. The pastry may not be quite as crispy, having been baked from frozen, but it will still be very good. The best way to bake the tarts from frozen is to turn on your oven to 180°C/Gas 4, as in the recipe overleaf, but instead of waiting for it to heat up, put the tarts in straight away. As the oven comes up to temperature, it will be defrosting the tarts, and they will bake through evenly without colouring too quickly. They will probably take a little longer – around 30 minutes – though this can vary, depending on how quickly your oven heats up, so keep an eye on them. You can check that they are baked all the way through by inserting a skewer into the middle and checking that it is hot. Turn up the heat to 200°C/Gas 6 for the last 5 minutes or so, just to get the pastry cream nicely coloured.

Make the pastry, then rest it in the fridge for at least 1 hour, preferably several, or, better still, overnight (see page 29).

To make the almond cream, beat the butter until very soft, preferably in a mixer. With the motor running, add the sugar and ground almonds and mix some more. Now mix in the flour, then the eggs, and finally the alcohol. Transfer to a small bowl and put in the fridge for 15 minutes.

Meanwhile, preheat the oven to 180°C/Gas 4.

Lightly grease four 16 cm rings or loose-bottomed tins (2 cm deep).

Skim a fine film of flour over your work surface, roll out the pastry 5 mm thick and use to line the tins (see pages 30–34). Place in the fridge to rest for at least 30 minutes then remove and fill with the almond cream. I like to do this with a piping bag, but you can spoon it in and smooth the surface if you prefer.

Top with the flaked almonds, place on baking trays and bake for 20 minutes, until golden brown. Leave in the tins for about 15 minutes.

Trim off the overhanging pastry then lift out and cool on a rack. Either dust with icing sugar, or brush with apricot glaze (see pages 105–106).

1 quantity Sweet or Almond Pastry (see page 17)

butter or baking spray, for greasing the tins

1 quantity almond cream (see page 119)

about 200 g clear apricot jam, for the glaze (optional)

rosemary sprigs, for decoration

For the poached peaches

500 g granulated sugar

2 sprigs rosemary

10 peaches

Peach & rosemary almond tarts

Peach and rosemary might sound like an unusual combination, but the flavours of the fruit and herb work really well together – though you could substitute some sprigs of thyme or lavender if you prefer.

Granulated sugar is much cheaper than caster sugar, and is fine for making things such as syrups. The syrup used to poach the peaches in this recipe can be stored in the fridge and simply boiled again when you want to use it for another recipe. Remember to skim off any impurities that come to the surface, and add a little water if the syrup needs to be thinner. It can also be used instead of apricot jam to glaze the tarts (see Variation).

If you wish, you can fill the pastry cases with almond cream, then freeze them, ready to bake. Alternatively, you can bake them, then freeze, defrost and warm them through (see page 119) before poaching the peaches.

Make the pastry, then rest it in the fridge for at least 1 hour, preferably several, or, better still, overnight (see page 29).

To make the poaching syrup, put the sugar and 2 rosemary sprigs in a pan with 1 litre water and bring to the boil. Lower the heat and simmer until you have a colourless syrup.

Put the whole peaches into the syrup, bring to just below a simmer, then cook very gently for 20 minutes. Take off the heat and leave to cool.

Lightly grease four 16 cm loose-bottomed tart tins (2 cm deep).

Skim a fine film of flour over your work surface, roll out the pastry 5 mm thick and use to line the tins (see pages 30–34). Place in the fridge to rest for at least 30 minutes.

Preheat the oven to 180ºC/Gas 4.

Using a spoon or piping bag, fill the pastry cases with the almond cream, then place on baking trays and bake for about 30 minutes, until golden. Leave in the tins for about 15 minutes, then lift out and cool on a rack.

Remove the peaches from the syrup (keep this to one side), peel the fruit, then cut in half carefully, as they can be a bit fragile. Remove and discard the stone.

With a skewer, make small holes in the baked almond cream and gently pour about 1–2 tablespoons of the syrup over each tart so it soaks in.

If making the apricot glaze, put the jam into a pan with a tablespoon or two of water and bring to just under a simmer – don't let it boil or the jam will become too gooey to spread properly. Alternatively, make the syrup glaze below. Using a pastry brush, lightly glaze the top of the tarts: this will give the fruit something to stick to. Place 5 peach halves on top of each tart, cut side downwards, then glaze a bit more. Push small sprigs of rosemary into the fruit to decorate.

Variation

Poaching syrup glaze: Put 200 ml syrup into a small pan, bubble it up to reduce a bit, then take off the heat. Soak 2 gelatine leaves in cold water for a few minutes, then squeeze them out and put into a cup or bowl. Add a little of the hot syrup and stir until the gelatine has dissolved, then mix into the rest of the syrup. Leave to cool, then brush over the tarts.

Makes 24 x 8 cm tarts

1 quantity Sweet Pastry (see page 17)

butter or baking spray, for greasing the tins

1 quantity almond cream (see page 119)

For the poached pears

500 g sugar

12 small ripe pears or 6 large ones, preferably Williams
or Comice

200 g clear apricot jam, for the glaze (optional)

Pear bourdaloue

There are many stories about how this got its name. The most likely is that it is named after La Pâtisserie Bourdaloue on rue Bourdaloue in Paris, where the recipe is said to have first been made in the early 1900s.

People often ask me how to make these classic pear tarts, filled with beautifully soft fruit, as you see them in virtually every French boulangerie/patisserie. The secret of the soft fruit is that they are usually made with tinned pears. That's not so surprising when you remember that fresh pears are only in season during the autumn. The tinned ones are fine, but when the fresh ones are around, I like to poach them in syrup, as in this recipe. The syrup can then be stored in the fridge and reused for both poaching and glazing (see page 124).

The recipe is for 24 small tartlets, but if you don't have that many tins, you can bake them in batches and freeze them until needed. Then you can defrost them and warm them through, ready for glazing. Make the pastry, then rest it in the fridge for at least 1 hour, preferably several, or, better still, overnight (see page 29).

Bring the sugar and 1 litre water to the boil in a pan, then simmer until you have a colourless syrup.

Peel the pears, keeping them whole, and put them into the syrup. Simmer gently for 20 minutes, then take off the heat and leave to cool.

Lightly grease 24 loose-bottomed tins, 8 cm in diameter and 2 cm deep. (If you don't have this many tins, you can bake in batches.)

Skim a fine film of flour over your work surface, roll out the pastry 2–3 mm thick and use to line the tins (see pages 30–34). Place in the fridge to rest for at least 30 minutes.

Preheat the oven to 180ºC/Gas 4. Halve the pears if small, or cut them into quarters if large. Place them rounded side up on the chopping board, then make several widthways cuts that go about two-thirds of the way through the flesh. Press down gently and the pear will fan out a little.

Remove the tins from the fridge and using a spoon or piping bag, half-fill each pastry case with the almond cream. Arrange a halved pear on top.

Place on baking trays and bake for about 25 minutes, until the almond cream is golden. Leave in the tins for about 15 minutes, then lift out and cool on a rack.

If making the apricot glaze, put the jam into a pan with a tablespoon or two of water and bring to just under a simmer – don't let it boil or the jam will become too gooey to spread properly. Using a pastry brush, lightly glaze the top of the tarts.

1 quantity Sweet Pastry (see page 17)

250 g sugar

6 rhubarb sticks, cut into 6–8 cm lengths

butter or baking spray, for greasing the tins

1 quantity almond cream (see page 119)

2 capfuls crème de cassis

1 punnet white currants

about 200 g clear apricot jam, for the glaze (optional)

Rhubarb & white currant tarts

This is a very simple but chic combination: the pink of the rhubarb and pearly white 'necklace' of currants give it quite a feminine appeal. Lightly poached rhubarb is a favourite of mine, and the recipe came about when I had some of the early season, bright pink, forced rhubarb (a speciality of West Yorkshire) in the kitchen, and decided to use it as a topping for an almond tart. I felt that an extra flavour and colour was needed so I added some white currants that I also happened to have to hand. It has become one of my favourite tarts. If you wish, you can fill the pastry cases with almond cream, then freeze them, ready to bake. Alternatively, you can bake and then freeze them until needed. Just defrost and warm them through (see page 119) before poaching the rhubarb. You can use the poaching syrup for a glaze (see page 124).

Make the pastry, then rest it in the fridge for at least 1 hour, preferably several, or, better still, overnight (see page 29).

Put the sugar and 500 g water into a pan and bring to the boil, stirring to dissolve the sugar. Lower the heat and simmer for about 20 minutes, until you have a colourless syrup.

Add the rhubarb and cook for 4–5 minutes, until it has softened but still offers resistance when you prod it with a sharp knife.

Using a slotted spoon, transfer the rhubarb to a rack placed over a baking tray to drain and cool. Set aside the pan of poaching syrup.

Preheat the oven to 180°C/Gas 4.

Lightly grease four 16 cm loose-bottomed tart tins (2 cm deep), preferably fluted.

Skim a fine film of flour over your work surface, roll out the pastry 5 mm thick and use to line the tins (see pages 30–34). Place in the fridge to rest for at least 30 minutes.

Using a spoon or piping bag, fill the pastry cases with the almond cream, then place on baking trays and bake for about 30 minutes, until golden. Leave in the tins for about 15 minutes, then lift out and cool on a rack.

Mix the crème de cassis with an equal quantity of the poaching syrup. Prick the top of the tarts with a skewer, then pour the liquid over the almond cream, letting it soak in. Arrange the fruit on top.

If making the apricot glaze, put the jam into a pan with a tablespoon or two of water and bring to just under a simmer – don't let it boil or the jam will become too gooey to spread properly. Using a pastry brush, lightly glaze the top of the tarts.

Makes 8 x 10 cm tarts

1 quantity Sweet Pastry (see page 17)

50 ml rum

2 litres cider

50 ml Calvados

6 heaped tbsp brown sugar

6 eating apples

butter or baking spray, for greasing the tins

1 quantity almond cream (see page 119), but made with Calvados rather than Poire William or rum

Tarte Normande

This is really two recipes in one. Every year at home we make a hot punch for Christmas, which is also brilliant for poaching apples for Tarte Normande – and then for drinking with a slice of it.

If you wish, you can make the tarts up completely, then freeze them until you are ready to bake. Alternatively, you can bake and then freeze them until needed. Just defrost and warm them through (see page 119) before serving.

I like to eat Tarte Normande at room temperature with crème fraîche, but sometimes I also pour a little warmed Calvados over the tart just before serving, which makes it extra special.

Make the pastry, then rest it in the fridge for at least 1 hour, preferably several, or, better still, overnight (see page 29).

Pour the alcohol into a pan, add the sugar and warm up on the hob, just as if you were making a hot punch or mulled wine – the alcohol shouldn't even bubble. Put in the apples, unpeeled and quartered, and let them sit in the punch over the lowest heat for several hours so that they soften and soak up the flavours.

Lightly grease eight 10 cm loose-bottomed tart tins (2 cm deep).

Skim a fine film of flour over your work surface, roll out the pastry 2–3 mm thick and use to line

the tins (see pages 30–34). Place in the fridge to rest for at least 30 minutes.

Preheat the oven to 180°C/Gas 4.

Using a spoon or piping bag, fill the pastry cases with the almond cream. Lift the apples from the punch, halve and core them, and slice thinly. Arrange the apple slices in a circular fashion.

Place on baking trays and bake for 20–25 minutes, until the almond cream is golden brown. Leave in the tins for about 15 minutes, then lift out and cool on a rack to room temperature before eating.

Makes 8 x 10 cm tarts

1 quantity Sweet Pastry (see page 17)

butter or baking spray, for greasing the tins

about 24 prunes in rum

1 quantity almond cream (see page 119)

2 tbsp flaked almonds

Prune & rum tarts

In my kitchen I always have big jars of prunes soaked in rum. They make great treats to serve with coffee during the morning break in pastry classes; and everyone who stops by the kitchen falls in love with them too. If I can escape for a day's fishing or shooting at the weekend, the gamekeeper always appreciates a jar of them; and a spoonful added to porridge in the morning is a fantastic wake-up call.

All you do is put a big bag of ready-to-eat prunes into a clean jar, add enough good dark Navy rum to cover, then leave for at least a week, topping up with more prunes as you eat them, or more rum as you drink it.

When making vanilla ice cream, I sometimes pop in a few of the prunes towards the end of churning, and the softest ones, squashed into sweet pastry cases, topped with almond cream and then baked, make beautiful tarts.

If you wish, you can make the tarts up completely, then freeze them until you are ready to bake. Alternatively, you can bake and then freeze them until needed. Just defrost and warm them through (see page 119) before serving.

Make the pastry, then rest it in the fridge for at least 1 hour, preferably several, or, better still, overnight (see page 29).

Lightly grease eight 10 cm loose-bottomed tart tins (2 cm deep).

Skim a fine film of flour over your work surface, roll out the pastry 2–3 mm thick and use to line the tins (see pages 30–34).

Place in the fridge to rest for at least 30 minutes.

Preheat the oven to 180°C/Gas 4.

Squash some of the prunes into each pastry case, then cover with almond cream and sprinkle with flaked almonds. Place on baking trays and bake for 25–30 minutes, until the almond cream is golden. Serve warm with crème fraîche.

Makes 36 tartlets or 1 large tart

1 quantity Pistachio Pastry (see page 17)

butter or baking spray, for greasing the tins

½ quantity almond cream (see page 119)

½ quantity crème pâtissière (see page 105)

about 200 g clear apricot jam, for the glaze

2 punnets raspberries

50 g ground pistachios, to finish

Raspberry & pistachio tarts

While these tarts are simple to make, the bright green from the pistachios and the red of the raspberries make them look quite spectacular and summery – one big, tart also looks pretty dramatic, if you prefer.

If you wish, you can fill the pastry cases with almond cream, then freeze them, ready to bake. Alternatively, you can bake and then freeze them until needed. Just defrost and warm them through (see page 119). Let them cool before adding the raspberries and pistachios.

Make the pastry, then rest it in the fridge for at least 1 hour, preferably several, or, better still, overnight (see page 29).

Lightly grease three 12-hole tart tins (if you don't have enough tins, bake in batches), or a square tin, 19.5 x 2.5 cm.

Lightly flour a work surface and roll out the pastry 2–3 mm thick for tartlets or 5 mm thick for a large tart. Use it to line your tins (see pages 33–36), then put into the fridge to rest for 30 minutes.

Preheat the oven to 180ºC/Gas 4.

Mix the almond cream and crème pâtissière together in a bowl. Using a spoon or piping bag, fill the pastry case(s) to the top with the mixed cream. Bake the tartlets for 15–20 minutes and the large tart for 25–30 minutes, until golden brown.

Leave to cool in the tin(s) for 15 minutes before lifting out and cooling on a rack.

Put the jam into a pan with a tablespoon or two of water, and bring to just under a simmer – don't let it boil or the jam will become too gooey to spread properly. Using a pastry brush, lightly glaze the top of the tart(s).

To decorate tartlets, sprinkle the tops with ground pistachios, then glaze lightly. Place a row of raspberries down the middle (see picture) and lightly glaze again.

To decorate a large square tart, arrange lines of raspberries in the centre and sprinkle a border of ground pistachios all around them. Lightly glaze again.

Makes 36

1 quantity Sweet Pastry (see page 17)

butter or baking spray, for greasing the tins

1 x 400 g jar luxury mincemeat

1 quantity almond cream (see page 119)

flaked almonds, to decorate (optional)

icing sugar, to dust

Frangipane mince pies

I had never seen anything like mince pies when I was growing up in France, but I absolutely love them. My only complaint is that they are often made with too much pastry in relation to the filling, so one Christmas I experimented with covering the pies instead with frangipane (almond cream) flavoured with rum and topped with flaked almonds. They went down such a treat that we now make batches of them to sell in our bakery in Bath, and also in the Saturday shop at the cookery school, and I can barely keep up with the demand.

The baked pies can be made 2–3 months in advance and frozen between layers of greaseproof paper in a plastic freezer box until Christmas. They can then be defrosted and warmed at 170°C/Gas 3 for 6–7 minutes to heat through, or eaten at room temperature.

Make the pastry, then rest it in the fridge for at least 1 hour, preferably several, or, better still, overnight (see page 29).

Lightly grease three 12-hole tart tins (if you don't have enough tins, bake in batches).

Lightly flour a work surface and roll out the pastry 2–3 mm thick. Using a round cutter or tumbler just larger than the holes in the tin, cut out circles of pastry and use to line your tins (see page 33). Put into the fridge to rest for 30 minutes.

Preheat the oven to 180°C/Gas 4.

Half-fill the pastry cases with mincemeat, then pipe about a heaped teaspoon of almond cream over each one. (Alternatively, spoon it on and smooth over the top.) Sprinkle with a few flaked almonds if you like.

Bake for about 25 minutes, until golden brown. Leave in the tins for about 15 minutes, then lift out and cool on a rack. Dust with icing sugar.

A Boxful of Sweet Biscuits

Sweet pastry can easily be adapted to make a range of biscuits. The recipes on pages 140–147 are quick to put together, and the resulting biscuits will keep for 2–3 weeks in an airtight container – though I never understand how anyone manages to make them last that long. In my family, the moment they are made they are gone! When you bake biscuits, instead of using greased baking trays, you might want to try silicone mats, which are perfect for the job.

Makes 24–36, depending on cutter size

1 quantity Sweet Pastry, or any variation of your choice (see page 17)

butter or baking spray, for greasing the baking trays

1 egg, beaten with a pinch of salt, for glazing

Everyday biscuits

There is no rule about which pastry dough to use for these biscuits – they can be made in all kinds of flavours and shapes. If you are using the basic sweet pastry dough, you could mix some chocolate chips or pieces of candied peel into it just before resting it. If you are using one of its variations, such as the chocolate pastry dough, you could add some flaked almonds or pieces of walnut. It really is up to you. Similarly, although the biscuits shown (far left in the picture on page 138) are square, you can use whatever shaped cutters you like, so they are fun to make with children.

Make the pastry dough, then rest it in the fridge for at least 1 hour, preferably several, or, better still, overnight (see page 29).

Preheat the oven to 180°C/Gas 4 and grease two baking trays.

Lightly flour a work surface and roll out the pastry 2 mm thick if you want thin biscuits, or 3–4 mm if you prefer them a little thicker. Cut into squares of about 6–7 cm, or use a similar-sized cutter to stamp out whatever shape you like. Dust off any excess flour with a pastry brush, then place on the prepared trays and brush with the beaten egg. Bake for 12–15 minutes, depending on the shape and thickness, until golden.

Makes about 24

1 quantity Sweet Pastry (see page 17), but add the zest of 2 oranges or the zest of 1 orange and a few drops of orange flower essence

butter or baking spray, for greasing the baking trays

1 egg, beaten with a pinch of salt, for glazing

1 quantity chocolate crème patissière (see page 208)

Orange & chocolate biscuits

These are little sandwiches of orange-flavoured biscuit filled with chocolate crème patissière (see page 208). You can make the biscuits and keep them for 2–3 weeks in an airtight container before sandwiching them with the filling, but once you add the crème patissière, you need to eat them on the same day.

The biscuits (centre in the picture on page 138) are flavoured, either with orange zest, or a combination of zest and orange flower essence.

Make the pastry dough, adding the orange zest with the flour. If using orange flower essence, mix it in after adding the butter. Rest the dough in the fridge for at least 1 hour, preferably several, or, better still, overnight (see page 29).

Preheat the oven to 180°C/Gas 4. Lightly grease one or two baking trays.

Lightly flour a work surface and roll out the pastry 2 mm thick if you want thin biscuits, or 3–4 mm if you prefer them a little thicker. Cut into an equal number of squares of about 6–7 cm, or use a similar-sized cutter to stamp out whatever shape you like. Dust off any excess flour, then place on the prepared trays and brush with the beaten egg. Bake for 12–15 minutes, depending on the shape and thickness, until golden. Sandwich the squares with the chocolate crème patissière.

Makes about 24

1 quantity Sweet Pastry (see page 17), but omit the salt, add 20g baking powder, 250g salted butter instead of 125g unsalted, and 3 egg yolks instead of 2 eggs and 1 yolk

butter or baking spray, for greasing the baking trays

1 egg, beaten with a pinch of salt, for glazing

Breton biscuits

I grew up in Brittany with biscuits like these (top right in the picture on page 138), made with local salted butter. They are gorgeous, made using the basic sweet pastry method, but with double the quantity of butter. You need a good butter flavoured with sea salt. I use Breton butter, made with sea salt flakes, which is just beautiful and you can find in most good shops and supermarkets. I also put a little baking powder in with the flour for this recipe, so the biscuits rise very slightly, and use only egg yolks rather than whole eggs. (You can use the leftover egg whites in the Italian Biscuits, at the end of this chapter.)

Make the pastry dough in the usual way, adding the baking powder to the flour, and rest in the fridge for at least 1 hour, preferably several, or, better still, overnight (see page 29). As you are using double the quantity of butter, the dough needs a long time to set.

Lightly grease two baking trays. Flour a work surface and roll out the dough 3–4 mm thick. Use a 6–8 cm round cutter or upturned glass to stamp out circles. Brush off any excess flour, then place on the prepared trays and brush with the beaten egg. Using a fork, make wavy patterns on the top of each biscuit, then put into the fridge for 30 minutes to firm up again before baking.

Preheat the oven to 180°C/Gas 4. Bake the biscuits for 12–15 minutes, until golden.

Makes about 24 fingers

1 quantity Sweet Pastry (see page 17), but use only 1 egg yolk rather than 2 eggs and 1 yolk, and add 60 g semolina to the flour

Shortbread

Everyone loves shortbread, and it is so easy to make – just one step beyond the rubbing-in stage for Sweet Pastry. Then all you have to do is press the crumbly mixture into a baking tin and put it into the oven. That's it! I usually cut the slab of shortbread into classic finger shapes, which means none of it is wasted, but you could use a cutter to stamp out shapes of your choice if you prefer.

Preheat the oven to 150°C /Gas 2 and line a deep, lipped baking tray (roughly 24 x 18 cm) with baking paper.

Make the pastry dough in the usual way, adding the semolina when you add the flour (see pages 18–21) but continue to work the butter into the flour until the mixture resembles fine breadcrumbs.

Add the sugar and the egg yolk. The mixture will be crumbly and a little sticky, like the topping for a fruit crumble. Transfer to the lined baking tray and press down gently, easing the mixture into the edges and corners so that you have a flat layer

about 1.5 cm deep. Prick all over with a fork, then bake for 45–50 minutes. When it is ready, the shortbread should be very lightly coloured, and if you lift up the baking paper towards the middle of the sheet, the shortbread should hold together and not break.

Remove the tin from the oven and leave to cool a little. Carefully lift out the shortbread, still on the baking paper, and use a sharp knife to cut it widthways into 12 slices 2 cm wide. Cut in half across the middle so that you end up with 24 fingers.

Makes about 36–40

300 g icing sugar, plus a little extra for rolling out

300 g ground almonds

2 tsp honey

3 egg whites

butter or baking spray, for greasing the baking trays

leftover apricot jam, crème patissière or flaked almonds (see page 105), to finish

Italian biscuits

Think of this as another bonus recipe. It is a variation on amaretti and although it doesn't follow the usual sweet pastry method, it is perfect for using up any egg whites, crème patissière or apricot glaze left over from other recipes.

Mix the icing sugar and ground almonds together. Add the honey and egg whites and mix until you have a smooth, firm dough. Leave to rest in the fridge for at least 30 minutes.

Preheat the oven to 150°C/Gas 2 and lightly grease two baking trays.

Divide the dough into four equal pieces. Dust a work surface with icing sugar and roll each piece of dough into a rough sausage shape. Slice each sausage into 8–10 equal pieces.

Lay these rounds of dough on the prepared baking trays, then gently press your thumb into the centre of each so that it leaves an indent. Fill the indents with a little jam, crème patissière or flaked almonds. Bake for around 15 minutes.

To test that the biscuits are ready, take the trays out of the oven and tap them lightly on a work surface. The biscuits should release themselves from the trays. Leave to cool.

110 g butter, softened and cut into pieces

zest of 1 lemon or orange

110 g caster sugar

3 egg whites (120 ml)

110 g plain flour

1 drop vanilla extract

Langues de chat

Like the previous recipe, this one also makes good use of egg whites left over from making pastry. These classic fine, crisp biscuits take their name from their shape, which is supposed to resemble a cat's tongue, and they are really simple to make.

Take the butter out of the fridge in advance to soften it, or use the rolling pin method (see page 18), rather than put it in the microwave and risk it becoming oily.

Preheat the oven to 150°C/Gas 2 and grease two baking trays.

In a bowl, beat the butter with the lemon or orange zest until soft. Add the sugar and continue to beat until pale and creamy, scraping the mixture from the sides of the bowl as you do so. Gradually beat in the egg whites and, finally, the flour, until you have a smooth paste. Stir in a drop of vanilla extract and rest the mixture in the fridge for at least 2 hours.

You can either pipe the mixture, which gives neatly shaped biscuits, or you can spoon it, which will give more interesting, slightly uneven shapes. It is up to you. If you decide to pipe the mixture, fill a piping bag fitted with a very small nozzle (see page 61) and pipe strips of about 6–7 cm (or longer if you prefer) onto your prepared trays. Leave a

finger-width space between each strip, as once the mixture is in the oven, it will spread out.

If you prefer to use a spoon, place about half a teaspoon of the mixture on a prepared tray and use the back of the spoon to spread it into a strip about 1 mm thick. Repeat this step with the rest of the mixture, leaving a finger-width space between the strips. Don't worry about the shape – the mixture will form its own in the oven.

Bake for 10–12 minutes, or until the centre of the biscuits is pale golden and the edges a darker golden. Remove the trays from the oven, but leave the biscuits in place for a few minutes before lifting off with a small palette knife, and cooling on a wire rack.

4 Puff

The key to baking with puff pastry is not to be scared to let it get dark golden brown so that it is really crispy and the butter inside it takes on a lovely nutty flavour. Pale, soggy puff pastry is always a disappointment.

When you use puff pastry for tarts or something delicate, such as millefeuilles, you need to prick the pastry with a fork in order to deflate some of the air pockets and stop it from rising up too much. It might seem odd to do this after spending so much time creating layers of pastry and air, but even when puff pastry is baked wafer thin and flat, it retains a light flakiness that is completely different from the sweet pastry in the previous chapter.

I hope that you will enjoy making your own puff pastry, but if you don't have the time or the inclination, choose a good all-butter ready-made one.

Makes 12 (6 of each flavour)

butter or baking spray, for greasing the baking trays

1 quantity Puff Pastry (see page 44) or 500 g good ready-made butter puff pastry

100 g Gruyère or Emmenthal cheese, grated

1 egg, beaten with a pinch of salt, for glazing the pastry

For the béchamel sauce

50 g unsalted butter

40 g plain flour

400 ml milk

sea salt and freshly ground pepper

freshly grated nutmeg, to taste

For the mushroom filling

knob of butter

about 6 small mushrooms, quartered

1 parsley sprig, chopped

For the bacon topping

6 slices of good bacon

Bacon or mushroom slices

A selection of these savoury slices, warm from the oven, is great for putting out with coffee in the morning. If you want to make only one flavour, just increase the quantities accordingly. The slices can be made up in their entirety to the point of baking and then frozen. Just defrost them and bake as usual.

Preheat the oven to 200°C/Gas 6 and grease two baking trays.

First make the sauce. Melt the butter in a heavy-based pan over a medium heat. When it is bubbling gently, take off the heat, add the flour and whisk briskly, until all the butter is absorbed and you have a paste that comes away cleanly from the pan.

Add the milk a little at a time, whisking continuously to avoid lumps. When the milk is all incorporated and the mixture is smooth, put the pan back onto a low–medium heat, stirring until the sauce starts to bubble. Cook for 1 minute more, then take off the heat. Season with salt, pepper and nutmeg to taste, then leave to cool.

If making the mushroom filling, melt the butter in a frying pan, add the mushrooms and fry gently for a couple minutes, until they colour a little. Take off the heat and stir in the parsley.

Skim a fine film of flour over your work surface, roll out the pastry 5 mm thick, then cut into 12 squares.

Fold two opposite corners of each square into the middle, then transfer the pastry slices to your prepared baking trays.

For bacon slices, spoon a little béchamel onto the pastry where the two corners meet, then add a slice of bacon and top with a little of the grated cheese.

For mushroom slices, mix the mushrooms with one-third of the béchamel in a bowl. Spoon some of this mixture onto the pastry where the two corners meet, then top with a little of the grated cheese

Brush the exposed areas of pastry with the beaten egg and bake in the oven for 12–15 minutes, until golden brown and crispy underneath.

Makes 36

butter or baking spray, for greasing the baking trays

1 chorizo ring

1 quantity Puff Pastry (see page 44) or 500 g good ready-made butter puff pastry

1 egg, beaten with a pinch of salt, for sealing the pastry

Chorizo bites

These circles of pastry with a slice of chorizo inside look like ravioli and are just the right one-mouthful size to serve (warm) with drinks. The easiest way to make them is to seal the slices of chorizo between two strips of pastry and then stamp out the little circles ready for baking. If you want to get ahead, you can make these up to the point of baking and then freeze them. Because they are so small, there is no need to defrost them – just bake as usual, though they may need five minutes or so in the oven to ensure they are heated all the way through.

Preheat the oven to 200°C/Gas 6 and grease two baking trays.

Cut the chorizo into 36 slices about 1 cm thick.

Skim a fine film of flour over your work surface, then roll out the pastry into a rectangle about 20 x 16 cm. Cut this lengthways into 4 equal strips about 4 cm wide.

Lay two of the strips horizontally in front of you. Place a line of 9 chorizo slices along the middle of each strip, leaving 2 cm between each slice, and a 2 cm space at either end.

Brush the exposed pastry around the chorizo slices with beaten egg, then cover with the remaining strips of pastry.

Now you need to seal the pastry around the chorizo. You can do this by pressing with your fingertips if they are delicate enough. If not, take a small pastry cutter, just a few millimetres larger than the chorizo, turn it upside down so you are not using the sharp side, then press it very gently around the chorizo to seal the pastry.

Now take a cutter a few millimetres larger, and this time use it the right way up to stamp out 9 circles, each with a slice of chorizo in the centre. Brush with beaten egg and, if you like, decorate the top by making little cuts with the tip of a knife (don't actually cut through the pastry).

Lay the circles on your prepared baking trays and put into the oven for about 15 minutes, until the pastry is crispy and golden. Cool for a few minutes before eating.

Makes 12 x 8 cm rolls or 24 cocktail-sized rolls

butter or baking spray, for greasing the baking tray

1 quantity Puff Pastry (see page 44) or 500 g good
ready-made butter puff pastry

1 egg, beaten with a pinch of salt, for sealing and glazing
the pastry

For the filling

300 g pork belly plus 300 g pork shoulder,
or 600 g minced pork

1 large onion, finely chopped

small bunch of curly parsley, finely chopped

50 g breadcrumbs

sea salt and freshly ground pepper

½ fresh nutmeg, grated

½ tsp ground allspice

Sausage rolls

Along with quiche, sausage rolls frequently get a bad press. Too often they are greasy or stodgy, or filled with bland-tasting sausage meat. But with properly made pastry and a homemade, well-seasoned filling, they are some of the best snack or party foods you can have. You can make them up to the point of baking, then freeze them, ready to defrost and bake as usual. Eat them warm or cold.

I make my sausage meat with half pork belly and half shoulder, which I mince myself, but if you like, you can just buy good-quality minced pork.

Preheat the oven to 200ºC/Gas 6 and grease a baking tray.

First make the filling. If mincing the meat yourself, use a food mixer with a medium mincing attachment. Mix the minced pork with the onion and parsley, then add the breadcrumbs and season with salt and pepper and the spices. To test that it is seasoned to your liking, take a little bit of the mixture and fry it in a pan until the meat is cooked through. Taste it and adjust the salt, pepper and spices as necessary.

Skim a fine film of flour over your work surface, then roll out the pastry into a rectangle 24 x 32 cm and 5 mm thick. Cut this lengthways into three long strips each 8 cm wide.

Spoon the sausage meat into a piping bag – a disposable bag is best for this, as you are using raw meat – then pipe a line of it along the length of each strip, just to the right of centre. Brush the long, right-hand edge of the pastry with beaten egg, then fold the opposite edge over to enclose the meat. Press together to seal. Cut widthways into four pieces if you are making large rolls, or into eight for cocktail rolls. Brush the tops with beaten egg.

Using a knife, score the top of each roll diagonally about 6–8 times, but don't cut all the way through the pastry. Place on your prepared baking trays and bake cocktail-sized rolls for 12–15 minutes, larger ones for 18 minutes, until the pastry is golden and crispy. Cool before serving.

Makes 1 x 28 cm tart

butter or baking spray, for greasing the tin/ring and baking tray

1 quantity Puff Pastry (see page 44) or 500 g good ready-made butter puff pastry

1 quantity crème patissière (see page 105)

½ quantity almond cream (see page 119)

12 fresh or canned apricots, drained if necessary

about 1 tsp caster or granulated sugar

about 200 g clear apricot jam, to glaze (optional).

Apricot tart

This is one of the first classic tarts you are taught how to make as an apprentice baker in France, and you learn the importance of allowing the pastry to become really dark golden brown so that it is properly crisp underneath. The apricot quarters become a little burnt at the tips, giving the tart real character. I still think it is one of the most beautiful of all tarts – crisp pastry, smooth vanilla crème patissière and the sweet tang of the apricots. It is perfect with no accompaniment whatsoever, except maybe a glass of sweet wine.

If you like, you can make this tart in exactly the same way using plums.

Preheat the oven to 200ºC/Gas 6 and grease a 28 cm loose-bottomed tart tin or ring/baking tray.

Skim a fine film of flour over your work surface, then roll out the pastry 4–5 mm thick and use to line your tin or ring (see page 34). Prick the base of the pastry with a fork.

Mix the crème patissière and almond cream together, then spoon into the pastry case, spreading it out evenly.

Cut the apricots in half, remove the stones, then cut in half again. Arrange these in a loose circular fashion on top of the creamy base, skin-side down, pushing one end of each slice gently into the cream, so that the other end points slightly upwards.

Sprinkle with the sugar. As the tart bakes, it will caramelise on the pointed ends of the apricots, which makes the tart look more attractive.

Place on a baking tray and bake for 12–15 minutes, then lower the heat to 180ºC/Gas 4 and bake for a further 20 minutes, until the apricots have caramelised and the pastry is dark golden. If you insert a table knife carefully under the edge of the pastry it should come away from the tin or ring. Leave in the tin for about 15 minutes, then lift out and cool on a rack.

You can leave the tart as it is, but if you want to give the apricots a little sheen, put the apricot jam into a pan with a tablespoon or two of water, and bring to just under the simmer – don't let it boil or the jam will become too gooey to spread properly. Using a pastry brush, lightly glaze over the apricots.

Makes 2 x 16 cm tarts

butter or baking spray, for greasing the tins/rings

1 quantity Puff Pastry (see page 44) or 500 g good ready-made butter puff pastry

1 quantity crème pâtissière (see page 105)

½ quantity almond cream (see page 119)

6–7 eating apples

about 200 g clear apricot jam, to glaze

For the apple compote

2 large Bramley apples

1 tbsp caster sugar or granulated sugar

splash of brandy

Apple tarts

If you are short of time or cooking apples to make the apple purée base for this recipe, you can use a small jar of good-quality apple compote, or puréed apple for babies. For the sliced apples, go for a good eating apple, such as a Cox or Braeburn, or a local or heritage variety that has a good balance of sweetness and sharpness. The tarts are good served either warm or at room temperature.

Preheat the oven to 200°C/Gas 6 and grease two 16 cm loose-bottomed tins or rings/baking trays.

First make the apple compote. Peel, core and chop the Bramleys, then put into a pan with the sugar, brandy and about a tablespoon of water. Simmer until the apple is just soft – about 15 minutes – then blitz to a purée using a blender. Leave to cool.

Skim a fine film of flour over your work surface, roll out the pastry 4–5 mm thick and use to line your tins or rings (see page 34). Prick the base of the pastry.

Mix together the crème pâtissière, almond cream and apple compote, then spread the mixture inside each pastry case.

Peel, core and finely slice the eating apples no more than 2 mm thick (see page 203). There are two different ways to arrange the apples: either place them in overlapping concentric circles, starting from the outside, with the rounded edges facing outwards (see picture); or simply overlap them in one circle around the outside, then arrange the last slices in a rosette in the centre (see picture and page 203).

Place on baking trays and bake for about 30–40 minutes, or until the apple and pastry are both golden brown and the tips of the apples are dark brown. The base of the tarts should be crispy, and you should be able to lift them cleanly from the baking tray with a fish slice.

Put the apricot jam into a pan with a tablespoon or two of water, and bring to just under the simmer – don't let it boil or the jam will become too gooey to spread properly. Using a pastry brush, lightly glaze the top of each tart. Eat warm or cold.

Makes 1 x 22 cm tart

1 quantity Puff Pastry (see page 44) or 500 g good ready-made butter puff pastry

6–8 eating apples, such as Cox or Braeburn

100 g good butter

200 g caster sugar

pinch of cinnamon

Tarte tatin

I'm sure everyone knows the story of how this tart is supposed to have been created accidentally by *les demoiselles* Tatin, the Tatin sisters, but in case you haven't… One of the sisters is said to have been softening apples in butter and sugar for an apple tart, then realised that she had left them in too long so they had caramelised and were sticking to the pan. She tried to rescue the situation by putting the pastry over the top, popping the pan into the oven, then turning the whole thing over to serve it. The guests at the hotel where the sisters worked apparently loved it. Whether the story is true or not, the tart has become one of the most famous desserts.

There is an assumption that tarte tatin is difficult to make, but when I teach people how to do it, they usually find that the only tricky part is turning the tart over when it has been baked. I think it helps to make it in a frying pan rather than in a tin because you can hold onto the handle to turn it over.

There are various schools of thought about how to make the tart. Some people slice the apples, others halve them, which is the way I prefer. Some people fill the pan with sugar then put in the apples, cover them with pastry and put the pan into the oven straight away, but this way you run the risk of the sugar becoming only a light, rather anaemic-looking caramel. I prefer something a bit darker and more toffee-like, so I start the tart off on the stove to get the caramel going. The key is to do this slowly and carefully so that the sugar doesn't get too dark, or even burn, and become brittle – more like toffee apple than tarte tatin, and not good for the teeth.

Choose eating apples that have a good balance of sweetness and sharpness, such as Cox, Braeburn or one of the characterful local or heritage varieties you can often find in farm shops or markets.

Preheat the oven to 200°C/Gas 6.

Skim a fine film of flour over your work surface, roll out the pastry until it is 4–5 mm thick and large enough to fit loosely in a 22 cm ovenproof frying pan. Prick the pastry well all over and either lay it on a large plate, or place a sheet of greaseproof paper over the top and roll it up, then put it into the fridge to rest while you prepare the apples and sugar.

Peel the apples, then cut in half from top to bottom and remove the cores.

Melt the butter in the frying pan over a medium heat. Sprinkle the sugar and cinnamon over it and cook gently for about 1 minute. Quickly arrange the apples, flat-side upwards, in the pan and keep over a medium heat, shaking it from time to time to ensure that the apples don't stick to the bottom. Don't worry if you can't fit in all the apples initially; they will shrink a little as they cook and you will be able to squeeze in more as necessary. You need to pack the apples tightly together so that the tart holds its shape when you turn it over.

Continue cooking gently and shaking the pan until the sugar turns to a rich caramel – this will take about 30 minutes. Remove the pan from the heat and rest it for 5 minutes.

Remove the pastry from the fridge and lay it loosely over the top of the apples. It needs to tuck in around the edge of the pan until it almost touches the caramel. The best way to do this without your fingers touching the caramel, which burns very badly, is to use the back of a teaspoon to nudge the pastry into place.

Bake for about 30 minutes, or until the pastry is really dark golden brown. Don't forget that when you flip the tart over after it is baked, the pastry is going to be the base, holding the apples and caramel together, so it needs to be really well coloured and crispy, otherwise it will become soggy with the juices from the apples.

Remove the pan from the oven and leave to cool for about a minute. This lets the caramel set a little and also makes it safer to turn out, but still take care as the caramel will still be hot.

To turn out, place a large plate over the pan and, holding both plate and pan firmly turn them over together so that the tart is apple-side up on the plate. You can serve the tart cold, but I think it is best warm, with crème fraîche or vanilla ice cream.

Variation

For a little twist to the classic recipe, I suggest you use a butter flavoured with sea salt; it will give a gorgeous salted caramel flavour to the tart.

Makes 1 x 20 cm galette

butter or baking spray, for greasing the baking tray

1 quantity Puff Pastry (see page 44) or 500 g good
ready-made butter puff pastry, cut in half

1 quantity almond cream (see page 119)

1 dried or ceramic bean (optional), to put inside the tart

1 egg, beaten with a pinch of salt, for glazing the pastry

100 g caster sugar or about 1 tbsp icing sugar

Galette des rois

The feast of Epiphany (6 January) is a special day in France and often marked by baking this traditional 'Kings' cake', named after the Three Kings. It is very simple: frangipane (almond cream) sandwiched between two rounds of puff pastry, with a dried (or ceramic) bean inside it. Whoever gets the slice with the bean is king (or queen) for the day. Nowadays, you can buy all sorts of porcelain figurines to put inside the cake instead of the bean. You just have to warn everyone to look out for something hard in case they break their teeth. In some families the tradition is that whoever is the king gets to choose their queen, or vice versa. In our family we used to have two cakes: a Kings' cake and a Queen cake, with a bean inside each one: more democratic!

Preheat the oven to 200°C/Gas 6 and grease a baking tray.

Skim a fine film of flour over your work surface and roll each piece of pastry into a circle about 4–5 mm thick and 20 cm in diameter. The exact size doesn't matter too much, as long as the circles are the same.

With a blunt knife, mark a border all the way around one circle about 5 mm in from the edge without cutting all the way through the pastry; alternatively, press the blunt side of a smaller size cutter lightly into the pastry. Prick the area of pastry inside the border with a fork. By doing this you stop the central area from puffing up too much, while letting the outer edge rise up to form a rim.

Lift the pastry base onto your baking tray and spread the almond cream over the pricked area. If you like, hide a bean somewhere inside the cream.

Brush the pastry rim with beaten egg, then lay the other circle of pastry on top. With your fingertips, press gently from the centre outwards to remove

any air pockets, then press the edges of the two circles together. With the back of a knife, decorate the top in a criss-cross pattern, then go around the edge, pushing the back of the knife into a pastry at intervals to give a scalloped effect.

Brush the top of the galette with two layers of beaten egg, then use your knife to make a small hole in the top of the pastry to allow steam to escape. Bake for about 25 minutes, turning the heat down to 180°C/Gas 4 halfway through the baking time. The pastry should be dark golden.

To finish off the galette you can glaze it in one of two ways. Put the caster sugar in a pan with 100 ml water, bring to the boil, then turn down the heat and simmer briefly until you have a light syrup. Brush this all over the top of the galette and leave to cool. Alternatively, sprinkle the top with icing sugar and put the galette back into the oven, just long enough for the sugar to melt and form a shiny glaze. Leave to cool before eating.

Makes 12

butter or baking spray, for greasing the baking trays

½ quantity crème patissière or crème légère (see page 105 or 211)

½ quantity almond cream (see page 119)

½ quantity apple compote (see page 161)

1 quantity Puff Pastry (see page 44) or 500 g good ready-made butter puff pastry

1 egg, beaten with a pinch of salt, for sealing the pastry

1 large eating apple or 2 small ones

caster sugar, for sprinkling

Apple & custard 'leftovers'

In France these pastries are known as *chaussons aux pommes* – *chaussons* are slippers, the kind of cosy slip-ons that are associated with grandads, and their apple namesakes are great comfort food. In England the usual name for these pastries is 'turnovers', but I call them 'leftovers' because they are a great way of using up any puff pastry, crème patissière, almond cream or apple compote that are left after you have made some of the other recipes in this book. When I was an apprentice in France, we never wasted anything, and used to mix up all three creams as they make a fantastic combination. However, if you don't have them all, you could combine just two, or even use them alone. Whatever filling is used, you will need around 450 g of it to one quantity of pastry.

The filled pastries can be frozen, ready to be defrosted and baked in the usual way when you need them.

Preheat the oven to 200°C/Gas 6 and grease two baking trays.

Mix the crème patissière, almond cream and apple compote together in a bowl.

Skim a fine film of flour over your work surface, roll out the pastry to 5 mm thick. Using a cutter or side plate about 10 cm in diameter, cut out 12 circles.

Brush the edges with the beaten egg, then spoon some of the cream mixture into the middle. Fold the pastry over itself to form a half-moon shape, then

press the edges together and crimp with a fork. Leaving the skin on the apple(s), slice them very thinly widthways through the core, so that you end up with 12 rings about 2 mm thick. Push out the pips, which will leave each slice with a star-shaped hole in the centre.

Brush each 'leftover' with beaten egg and lay a slice of apple on top. Sprinkle with a little caster sugar, then place on your prepared baking trays and bake for 20 minutes, until the base of each 'leftover' is golden brown.

Makes 5

butter or baking spray, for greasing the baking tray

1 quantity Puff Pastry (see page 44) or 500 g good ready-made butter puff pastry

a little rum

1 quantity crème patissière or crème légère (see page 105 or 211)

icing sugar, for sprinkling

Millefeuilles

The name of these means '1000 leaves', which is simply a way of describing this classic light pastry, with its multilayered pastry sandwiching layers of creamy filling. Millefeuille is one of the first things that would-be pastry chefs are taught at college, and the key is to get the right balance of pastry and filling. Too much of one or the other and you don't get the full, mouth-filling pleasure of the contrasting textures and flavours. Often I see mass-produced millefeuilles made with pale-looking, uninteresting pastry, overfilled with artificial-tasting cream, and smothered in coloured icing. I like to keep millefeuilles simple, elegant and classic, filled only with crème patissière or crème légère.

Preheat the oven to 200ºC/Gas 6 and grease a baking tray.

Skim a fine film of flour over your work surface, roll out the pastry to form a rectangle 30 x 20 cm and 4–5 mm thick. Place on your baking tray and prick well all over with a fork. Bake for 20 minutes until golden, then turn over very carefully, place a similar-sized baking tray on top to keep the pastry from rising, and return to the oven for 5–10 minutes, until golden brown. Remove and cool on a rack.

When cool, cut the rectangle of pastry lengthways into three strips about 10 cm wide. You will see that each strip has a flat side and a more bobbly side. Reserve the strip with the best flat side for the top. Of the other strips, lay one of them with the flat side downwards on your work surface. Mix the rum into the crème patissière or crème légère and spoon half of this down the centre (alternatively you can pipe it, see page 61). Don't spread it, or it

will ooze out once you put the pastry on top. Instead, just place the next strip of pastry on top, again flat side downwards, and press it down very gently. Spoon or pipe the rest of the cream as before, then top with your reserved strip of pastry: this time you want the flat side upwards.

To decorate the top, sprinkle with icing sugar. Then, if you like, take two metal skewers and put one over a gas ring to heat. Use this to carefully and lightly brand the sugar diagonally in one direction. While you are doing this, heat the second skewer and use it to do the same thing in the opposite direction so that you create a dark, criss-cross pattern in the sugar. If you don't have a gas hob, you could use a blow-torch to heat the skewers. If you don't have either, leave the icing sugar as it is.

Finally, with a sharp knife, carefully cut widthways into five slices, washing and drying the knife after each cut, so that you keep the slices looking neat.

Makes 12

butter or baking spray, for greasing the tin

icing sugar, for dusting

1 quantity Puff Pastry (see page 44) or 500 g good ready-made butter puff pastry

about 100 g icing sugar

1 quantity crème patissière (see page 105)

cinnamon or nutmeg (optional)

Natas (Portuguese custard tarts)

When I first came to London, I lived near Portobello Road, and it was always a treat to go to the Lisboa Patisserie for one of their famous and gorgeous Portuguese tarts. I say one, but the problem was you always wanted more.

Although I have called them custard tarts, I make my *natas* with crème patissière rather than custard (crème anglaise), which is baked until you get dark brown patches on top.

In France I had grown up eating *flan*, which is a similar kind of tart, but usually a big one cut into slices. The little, deep and irregular-shaped *natas* have a greater ratio of pastry to custard, and because you roll the pastry in sugar, it becomes caramelised in places: irresistible! You can finish the tarts off with a sprinkling of cinnamon or nutmeg if you like, though I prefer them plain.

Lightly grease a 12-hole muffin tin using a butter paper, or melt a little butter and brush it inside the holes. Even if you use a non-stick tin – unless it is brand new – it is worth doing this as the sugar on the pastry will caramelise and cling to any bits of the tin that have lost their non-stick properties.

Dust your work surface with icing sugar. Take the pastry from the fridge and roll out 4–5 mm thick, sprinkling well with more icing sugar as you go.

Use a pastry cutter to cut 12 rounds of pastry about 10 cm in diameter – they need to be big enough to line the holes and leave a little overhang (see page 33). Put the tin into the fridge to rest for about 1 hour.

Preheat the oven to 200ºC/Gas 6.

Remove the tin from the fridge and fill each pastry case with the crème patissière. Sprinkle with cinnamon or nutmeg, if using. Bake for 15–20 minutes, until the pastry is golden, the sugar it was rolled in is caramelised and the crème patissière is dark in spots. Allow to cool for just a few minutes before lifting the tarts out of the tin; don't leave them in much longer, or the caramelised sugar may weld the tarts to the tin. Leave to cool completely before eating.

Makes about 8

butter or baking spray, for greasing the baking tray

caster sugar or granulated sugar, for dusting/sprinkling

1 quantity Puff Pastry (see page 44) or 500 g good ready-made butter puff pastry

cinnamon (optional)

Palmiers

Traditionally, these French pastries are shaped like a palm leaf or a butterfly, but mine are more freestyle, and quite fun to make. Kids love doing them, and though, in my experience, they are usually gone the minute they have cooled down, they will keep in an airtight container for 3–4 days.

Preheat the oven to 180ºC/Gas 4 and grease a baking tray.

Skim a fine film of flour over your work surface, roll out the puff pastry until you have a square or rectangle about 5 mm thick, then cut it into 24 x 5–6 cm squares.

Sprinkle each square with a little sugar (and cinnamon if you like), then sit three squares on top of each other so that you have eight little stacks. Sprinkle some more sugar on top of each stack, then take a wooden spoon and press the length of the handle down diagonally across the top of each one so that it sinks in the centre and the edges lift up.

Place the palmiers on the prepared baking tray and bake for 10–15 minutes, or until golden and caramelised. They will puff up in different ways so they are quite quirky. Cool on a wire rack for 5 minutes.

Makes around 24

½ quantity Puff Pastry (see page 44) or 250 g good ready-made butter puff pastry

100 g icing sugar

about 80 g flaked almonds or ground pistachios or a few teaspoons sesame seeds or poppy seeds, or some of each

Croustillants

These are wafer-thin slices of puff pastry, coated in sugar and baked so that they are crunchy (*croustillant* is French for something crispy), and they are perfect for using up scraps of puff pastry left over from making tarts, sausage rolls, etc. You can sandwich them together with Chantilly cream (see page 181) and berries, or any fruit you like, to make a smart-looking dessert. However, I also like to encrust them in nuts or seeds, as in this recipe, and eat them like biscuits. Because any humidity in the air will affect their crispiness, croustillants are best made and eaten within a few hours.

Preheat the oven to 200°C/Gas 6 and line two baking trays with greaseproof paper.

Roll the puff pastry into a sausage shape about 24 cm long, then cut into 24 slices 1 cm thick.

Dust your work surface with icing sugar and place a piece of pastry on it, cut-side down. Sprinkle a little more icing sugar on top and, using a small rolling pin, roll the pastry into a long, roughly oval shape that is paper thin. Turn it over several times while rolling to coat it in the icing sugar and to

make sure that it doesn't stick. Repeat with the remaining pieces of pastry.

Lay the croustillants on the prepared baking trays and sprinkle the top of each with your chosen nuts or seeds – about a teaspoonful per croustillant. Place the tray on the middle shelf of the oven and bake for 6–8 minutes, until the croustillants are caramelised. Be sure to keep a close eye on them as they can burn quickly. Use a palette knife to lift them from the tray and cool on a wire rack.

5   Choux

Choux pastry is less of a dough, more of a batter, which is very easy to make and is used for all kinds of light savoury buns and sweet confections, such as cream puffs, profiteroles and éclairs. The moisture in the batter causes it to expand in the heat of the oven, and this creates a pastry that is hollow inside. Once it has cooled down, you can inject the cavity with anything from cream cheese and smoked salmon to sweet chantilly cream or crème patissière. Sweet buns are often glazed with chocolate (as in éclairs and profiteroles) or stacked up in a pyramid and drizzled with chocolate sauce, or swirled in spun sugar to make the classic French wedding cake, *croquembouche*.

There are two skills involved in making successful choux pastry. The first is becoming confident at using a piping bag so that you can create the shapes you want, from round buns to long, elegant éclairs, or the necks and bodies that can be assembled to make 'swans'. The second skill is baking the pastry properly so that it not only puffs up, but also dries out, which means that when you take it from the oven, it doesn't deflate and become limp, but provides a strong support for whatever you are going to pipe inside it.

Some people put sugar into the choux batter if it is going to be filled with cream or glazed with melted chocolate, but I prefer not to add sugar because it tends to prevent the pastry from drying out so well. Instead, I have just the one recipe for choux pastry, and it works for both savoury and sweet fillings.

Makes 12

butter or baking spray, for greasing the baking trays

1 quantity Choux Pastry (see page 56)

1 egg, beaten with a pinch of salt, for glazing

icing sugar, for dusting

For the chantilly cream

250 g whipping or double cream

2 tbsp caster sugar

a few drops of vanilla extract or rosewater (optional)

Swans

Yes, I know these are very 1970s, but we include them in the classes at our school because they offer a great way to become used to piping choux pastry, and people are fascinated to see how they are assembled, and very proud of themselves when they have made them.

The swan necks are the trickiest part because they are very delicate and fragile, which is why I suggest you pipe double the quantity you need, as up to half of them are likely to break when you lift them off your baking tray or silicone mat. Casualties are just a hazard of swan-making.

I use three different fabric piping bags for these. Two are filled with choux batter for piping the necks and bodies of the swans – one bag has a thin nozzle and the other a medium star-shaped nozzle. The third bag I use to pipe the chantilly cream, again with a medium star-shaped nozzle. You need three bags ready to go, as there is not time to wash and dry them in between piping, but you can of course use disposable bags.

The chantilly cream that forms the swans' feathers is also good for serving with fruit tarts.

 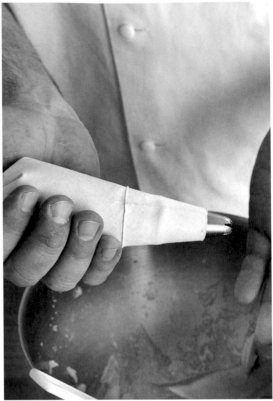

Preheat the oven to 170°C/Gas 3. Lightly grease two non-stick baking trays or have ready two silicone mats.

Prepare three piping bags: insert 1 cm star nozzles into two of them, and a plain nozzle with a tiny hole the size of a biro point into the third.

Take two piping bags – one with the fine nozzle and one with a star nozzle – and fill with the batter (see page 61).

To pipe, hold the bag in one hand with the other hand underneath to steady and guide it. Squeeze with the hand holding the bag, pipe, then turn the bag anticlockwise, squeeze again, applying the same pressure all the time, and pipe again. I have noticed that most people tend to hold the bag with one hand and squeeze with the other, but this doesn't give you the same control.

First make the swans' necks. Using the bag with the fine nozzle, pipe 24 thin 'S' shapes onto a prepared baking tray or mat.

Now change to the bag with the star nozzle and pipe the bodies onto a separate prepared tray or mat. Squeezing gently, pipe a rosette shape, then draw the bag towards you so that you end up with an elongated 'body' with a little tail. Repeat until you have 12 bodies.

Put the tray containing the necks into the oven and bake for 8–10 minutes, checking all the time to make sure they don't burn. They should be golden brown, but will go from beautifully golden to burnt very quickly if you don't keep an eye on them. Remove the tray from the oven and leave to cool.

Brush the tops of the bodies very lightly with the beaten egg – not so much that it drips onto the tray or mat. The bodies need to bake longer than the necks in order to dry out properly. They should take about 20 minutes, by which time they will be golden and puffed up. For the last 4 minutes of baking, leave the oven door slightly ajar to allow the steam to escape and help the drying process. Remove the tray from the oven and leave to cool.

To make the chantilly cream, whisk the ingredients together until thick, but be careful not to overwhisk or you will end up with butter rather than cream. Fill your third piping bag with the mixture.

Slice the top off each choux pastry body – the inside should be dry and hollow. Lay the tops, cut-side down, on your work surface and cut in half to make 'wings'.

Using a circular motion, pipe some of the cream into the cavity of each body. Gently insert a wing (shiny-side upwards) into the cream on each side.

With a scraper or small palette knife, carefully lift each swan neck from the baking tray and insert into the cream at the opposite end to the tail. Finally, very lightly dust the whole swan with a tiny amount of icing sugar. (The various stages are shown in the picture opposite.)

Makes about 12 medium éclairs, or 24 small ones

butter or baking spray, for greasing the baking tray

1 quantity Choux Pastry (see page 56)

1 quantity chantilly cream (see page 181)

200 g good-quality milk or dark chocolate (53% cocoa solids)

Chocolate éclairs

Eclairs are made in much the same way as the swans on page 181, but are a lot simpler, as you only need to pipe the choux pastry in straight lines.

The chocolate glaze is simply made by melting good chocolate. Unless you like a bitter edge to the flavour, you don't need a chocolate with a very high percentage of cocoa solids: 53% is fine.

Although I suggest chantilly cream for the filling as it is quite light and fluffy, you could also use crème patissière (see page 105). A classic bakery filling is crème patissière with a good dash of rum mixed into it. Or you could use chocolate or coffee crème patissière (see pages 208 and 209).

Preheat the oven to 170°C/Gas 3. Lightly grease a non-stick baking tray or have ready a silicone mat.

Fit a piping bag with a plain nozzle about 1 cm in diameter and fill with the choux batter (see page 61).

If making large éclairs, pipe 12 lines about 12–15 cm long onto your baking tray or mat. If making small eclairs, pipe 24 lines about 8 cm long.

Bake large éclairs for 15–20 minutes, and small ones for 12–15 minutes, until golden and puffed up. For the last 4 minutes of baking, leave the oven door slightly ajar to allow the steam to escape and help the drying process. Remove the tray from the oven and leave to cool.

There are two ways to fill the éclairs with the cream. You can either carefully cut them in half lengthways and pipe the cream inside, using a piping bag with a medium-sized star nozzle (about 1 cm diameter); or you can make a small hole at one end of the éclairs and squeeze cream into the hollow using a piping bag with a straight nozzle (about 5 mm in diameter).

If you want to glaze the éclairs with chocolate, it needs to be done at different times, depending on which method of filling you are using. Do it first and let it set if you are planning to cut the éclairs in half and fill them with cream; otherwise, you can do it after you have injected the cream.

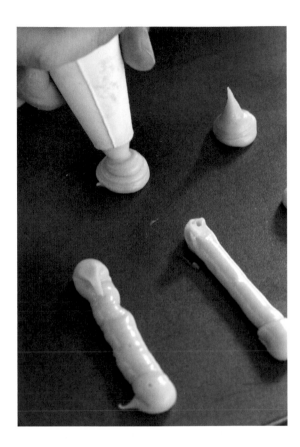

To make the glaze, break the chocolate into chunks and put into a heatproof bowl. Place this over a pan of simmering water – you need enough water to come close to the bottom of the bowl but not actually touch it. Turn the heat very low so that you don't get steam into the bowl, as this can make the chocolate stiffen and look dull. Let the chocolate melt slowly, stirring all the time. Remove from the heat.

If you are halving the éclairs, take the upper halves one by one and dip the tops into the chocolate. Let the excess drain off into the bowl, then place on a wire rack until the chocolate has set. You can then pipe the cream into the cavities of the bottom halves and put the chocolate-dipped halves on top.

If you are injecting cream inside the éclairs, you can do this before dipping them in the chocolate. Again, leave them on a rack until the chocolate sets.

Variation

You could also make the éclairs without the chocolate glaze on top, and simply halve and fill them with chantilly cream and fresh fruit. If you want to do this, lightly glaze the top of the unbaked strips with egg beaten with a pinch of salt, and run the prongs of a fork along it for decoration before baking. When the éclairs are filled, dust with icing sugar.

Makes at least 24

1 quantity Choux Pastry (see page 56)

1 egg, beaten with a pinch of salt, for glazing

about 8–10 cane sugar cubes, coarsely crushed, or 50 g chopped hazelnuts,

or use half quantities of each, mixed together

Chouquettes

These are little buns topped with crushed sugar and/or chopped hazelnuts. Because they are baked for quite a short length of time, they are slightly soft and chewy. If you like, though, you can leave them in the oven for a little longer in order to dry them out a bit more and keep them firmly puffed up. Then you can fill them with chantilly cream (see page 181) or crème patissière (see page 105). A great thing to do for a party is to arrange them in a pyramid on a big plate, melt some chocolate (see page 189) and spoon it over the top.

Preheat the oven to 170°C/Gas 3. Lightly grease a non-stick baking tray or have ready a silicone mat.

Fit a piping bag with a plain nozzle about 1 cm in diameter and fill with the choux batter (see page 61).

Pipe 24 dots onto your baking tray or mat (see picture, page 189). Brush the tops very thinly with beaten egg and sprinkle with the crushed sugar, chopped nuts, or a mixture of both.

Bake for 12–15 minutes, until golden and puffed.

For the last 4 minutes of baking, leave the oven door slightly ajar to allow the steam to escape and help the drying process. Remove the tray from the oven and leave to cool.

Makes 24–30

1 quantity Choux Pastry (see page 56)

100 g good strong Cheddar or Gruyère cheese, grated

vegetable oil, for deep-frying

smoked paprika, for dusting

Cheese puffs

You can bake these in the same way as Chouquettes (see opposite), but I like them best walnut-sized and deep-fried, then dusted in smoked paprika – great for serving with drinks.

Make the pastry in the usual way, then mix the cheese into the batter at the end.

Put some vegetable oil in a fryer or deep pan (making sure it comes no further than a third of the way up) and heat to 170ºC. If you don't have a thermometer, you can test if it is hot enough by dropping in a little of the choux mixture – it should sizzle.

Using a teaspoon, take walnut-sized pieces of the batter and ease them into the oil. Fry for 2–3 minutes, until puffed up and golden. Lift out with a slotted spoon, drain on kitchen paper and dust with smoked paprika.

Makes about 12 x 12 cm strips

250 g plain flour	5 g salt
½ tsp baking powder	20 g sugar
50 g unsalted butter	vegetable oil, for deep-frying
	caster sugar, for dusting

Churros

This is my final bonus recipe, which is made in a slightly different way from the basic choux pastry. In fact, it is rather like a variation on the hot-water crust recipe on page 85, but I just had to include it because I love churros. In Spain if you try to walk past one of the cafés that specialises in these strips of sugary doughnut, the smell of hot oil and sugar is just impossible to resist.

Traditionally, they are made using a *churrera*, a pump with a special nozzle, which squeezes the churro mixture into hot oil in long, snaking, ridged rings. Once these are fried, they are snipped into short lengths and dusted in sugar and sometimes cinnamon, ready for dipping into the thick hot chocolate that is usually served with them. At home you can use a piping bag, and snip the mixture into shorter, more manageable lengths as you pipe it into the oil. The secret is to fry them slowly at a relatively low temperature so that they get crispy on the outside, without burning, and are well-cooked all the way through, otherwise they can be stodgy.

Put the flour and baking powder into a bowl.

Put the butter, salt and sugar into a pan with 250 g or ml water. Bring to the boil and boil for 1 minute, then pour the mixture into the flour bowl, beating well until you have a thick batter.

Fit a piping bag with a big star nozzle about 1.5 cm in diameter and fill with the batter (see page 182).

Put some oil in a fryer or deep pan (making sure it comes no further than a third of the way up) and heat to 170°C. If you don't have a thermometer, you can test if it is hot enough by dropping in a little of the mixture – it should sizzle.

With one hand, pipe the mixture into the oil, using the other hand to snip it off every 10–15 cm with a pair of kitchen scissors. Fry for about 3–4 minutes, turning over regularly until the churros are golden on all sides. Lift out and drain briefly on kitchen paper.

Put the caster sugar on a large plate. While the churros are still hot, toss them in the sugar and serve with hot chocolate.

Variation

Instead of serving hot chocolate for dipping the churros into, you could make a little sauce with 100 g melted chocolate (see page 188) mixed with 2 tablespoons double cream.

6 Finishing touches

I am often asked how to present fruit tarts so that they look as artistic as the ones people have seen in the windows of pastry shops and bakeries when they are on holiday in France. Well the secret is really in the cutting of the fruit as much as the arrangement, so here are a few tricks and tips.

Strawberries

In a classic strawberry tart the fruit is laid on top of cream or crème patissière (see page 105). Make sure the berries are firm but ripe: remember, flavour is more important than appearance. Try to keep the size of your fruit in proportion with your tart(s): choose small berries for little tartlets. If you have tiny berries, or are using wild strawberries, which are usually very small, you can stand them upright, packing them close together. For little round tarts, begin with one upright strawberry in the centre, then pack the other berries around it, upright and in circles, working outwards. For little square tarts, you can arrange a line of upright berries along each side to make a border, then place the rest in upright lines within that.

For larger tarts, use bigger berries and cut them in half. If you are using just a few whole, halved or sliced strawberries on a mixed fruit tart, it can look more eye-catching if you leave the stalk and leafy hull on them; but if you are topping a tart only with strawberries, this can be a bit much, so remove them – carefully. If you tug at the stalk clumsily, the hull will come away, leaving a jagged hole, and the strawberries will end up looking like they have had a bite taken out of them. If necessary, use the point of a peeler or a pair of tweezers to help you remove the hull cleanly.

When you stand a strawberry upright with the hull at the top, you will see that it looks more bulbous at that end, so if you are halving or slicing the fruit, cut through the fattest part to get the best, most rounded heart-shape.

If you are using only strawberries on a large tart, start the arrangement in the middle of the tart with one halved berry, cut-side down, then work outwards in circles. Imagine you are tiling a roof and that the strawberry halves are tiles. Lay them, cut-side down and pointed ends towards the centre, slightly overlapping, round and round so that there are no gaps through which you can see the cream underneath.

Raspberries

As with strawberries, choose berries that are firm but ripe, and, if you like, combine yellow and white varieties as well as red ones. Keep raspberries whole and upright, with the tip (rather than the hollow) pointing upwards. If you are making a square tart, arrange the berries in rows. If you are making a round tart, start in the centre (as with strawberries), then work outwards in circles, packing the berries tightly together to hide the cream beneath. Alternatively, if you want a really dense, compact layer of raspberries, lay the berries on their sides rather than standing up, and push the tip of one into the hollow of the next so that they join together.

Stone Fruit

Fruits such as peaches and nectarines tend to be used freshly sliced on a base of cream or crème patissière, whereas apricots and plums, once arranged on a tart, are often baked. Sometimes they are even poached whole before being sliced in order to soften their texture. On a large tart, apricots or plums look impressive cut into quarters and arranged with the tips pointing upwards so that these blacken a little during baking and give definition to the pattern of fruit.

If you are slicing stone fruit, leave the skin on and cut in half before removing the stone. Provided the fruit is ripe, the stone should come out cleanly. Slice each half of the fruit thinly with a sharp knife, making half-moon shapes about 1–2 mm thick. These look most effective on round tarts because you can make a rose pattern with the slices of fruit. Start at the outer edge and, using the largest slices first, arrange them with the skin side facing upwards so that they overlap each other. Then work inwards, continuing to overlap the slices in concentric circles, and gradually moving on to the smaller slices. Keep a few of the very smallest for the centre and, when you reach it, arrange two, three or four slices (depending on the size of the tart), tightly overlapping each other, leaving just a small space in the very centre for the last slice. Curl this tightly round itself and place it upright in this space, so that it resembles the heart of a rose.

Apples

The key to producing neat-looking apple slices is to peel the fruit starting at the stalk end and go around the circumference. This will give you a nice rounded shape that can be sliced into neat half-moons. Peeling the fruit in strips from stalk to base might seem easier, but this gives a flatter, less rounded shape and produces angular slices.

The secret of successful peeling is to hold the peeler still and move the apple, not the other way round. In my classes people often get quite competitive about trying to take all the peel off in one strip – and I admit when I was an apprentice we used to do the same thing in the bakery – but it really doesn't matter if it takes one go or several.

Once the apples are peeled, use a small, sharp knife to cut each one in half and take out the core as neatly and sparingly as possibly. Try not to make a crater around it, as that is just a waste of apple.

Next, to slice your apple neatly and efficiently, put each half, flat-side down, on your work surface, with the cavity where the core used to be running from left to right. Slice downwards all the way across the apple half, keeping your cuts about 5 mm apart.

If you are making round tarts, arrange the apples either in circles or in a rose pattern (as for stone fruit, opposite).

Mixed Fresh Fruit Tarts

This is a chance to experiment and have fun on a cream or crème patissière base, mixing fruit such as kiwi and red or white currants with the more classical tart fruits such as berries and apricots.

Some people like to add a few rounds of banana – if you do this, be aware that the cut fruit will darken very quickly, so squeeze a little lemon juice over it. Also, if you are glazing the fruit with apricot jam (see opposite), make sure you cover the banana really well with it to prevent any discoloration.

Peel kiwi fruits neatly with a peeler, then slice into rounds, or cut in half lengthways before slicing so that you have half-moon shapes.

If you are using oranges, separate them into segments, but don't peel away the membrane or cut them as they will lose too much juice and begin to look dry very quickly.

Of course, you could keep each fruit separate, in lines or circles, but it is quite difficult to make fruits of different sizes and shapes look neat, so I prefer a looser approach. The important thing is to get some height, so I like to put in a few small bunches of red or white currants, and mix whole berries with slices of other fruits.

Usually, I begin by making a border all the way around, with overlapping slices of nectarines or peaches. Next, I might arrange some slices of kiwi and halved strawberries on top of the stone fruit, at intervals around the outside. If I am making a square tart, I would probably mark each corner with a halved strawberry and each side with a slice of kiwi. Although I don't normally recommend arranging strawberries cut-side up as they dry out quickly, they can look good, one in each corner, or dotted around the edge of a round tart, with the green hull left on and facing outwards. Once I have placed fruit around the borders, I will just make a 'picture' with the remaining fruit, packing it in to create a combination of different colours, heights and shapes. I find that the looser and less neat you try to be, the better.

Glazing

Glaze fresh fruits with clear, melted apricot jam (see page 105) to give the tart a professional-looking finish and sheen. The secret is just to melt the jam in a pan with 1–2 tbsp water, but don't let it boil or it will become gluey. Holding the pan with one hand and a wide brush in the other, dab the glaze onto the fruit gently and neatly; don't drag the brush or you will disturb the fruit. As the glaze cools, it will thicken again, so don't persevere with it or you will end up with lumps and dollops, which will ruin the look of your tart. Just put the pan back on the heat and warm up the glaze again so that you keep it fluid all the time.

Alternative Creams

Half the fun of making tarts is experimenting, not only with different fruits, colours and textures, but also with the flavours of the creams that you use as a base. Below are a few ideas.

Note: In all these creams, semi-skimmed milk could be used instead of full fat if you prefer, but the cream will not be as rich.

Makes about 400 ml

250 ml full-fat milk

1 vanilla pod

60 g caster sugar

2 tsp cocoa powder

3 egg yolks

25 g plain flour

Chocolate crème patissière

This is a variation on the classic crème patissière on page 105. Try it as an alternative base for Fruit Tartlets (page 105), as a filling for Millefeuilles (page 171) or Éclairs (page 188), or make your own experiments.

Put the milk into a heavy-based saucepan. Using a sharp knife, split the vanilla pod along its length, scrape the seeds into the milk, then put the pod halves in too. Add half the sugar and the cocoa powder.

Put the egg yolks and the rest of the sugar into a bowl and whisk until pale and creamy. Add the flour and mix until smooth.

Put the pan of milk over a medium heat, bring to just under the boil, then slowly pour half of it into the egg mixture, whisking well as you do so. Add the remainder of the milk and whisk again, then pour the mixture back into the pan. Bring

to the boil, whisking all the time, then keep boiling and whisking continuously for 1 minute. Take off the heat.

Pour the mixture into a clean bowl and scoop out the vanilla pods. (You can wash and dry them and keep them in a jar of sugar, which will give you vanilla-flavoured sugar for use in all your baking.) Cover the surface of the bowl with greaseproof paper straight away to prevent a skin forming. Allow to cool, then store in the fridge until you're ready to use it.

Makes about 400 ml

250 ml full-fat milk

1 heaped tbsp good ground coffee

3 egg yolks

60 g caster sugar

25 g plain flour

Coffee crème patissière

You could use this version of crème patissière to fill Éclairs or Chouquettes (page 188 or 192).

Put the milk and coffee into a heavy-based saucepan.

Put the egg yolks and sugar into a bowl and whisk until pale and creamy. Add the flour and mix until smooth.

Put the pan of milk and coffee over a medium heat and bring to just under the boil. Take off the heat and pass through a fine sieve into a jug or bowl, then slowly add half of it to the egg mixture, whisking well as you do so. Add the remainder of the milk and whisk again, then pour the mixture back into the pan. Bring to the boil, whisking all the time, then keep boiling and whisking continuously for 1 minute. Take off the heat.

Pour the mixture into a clean bowl and scoop out the vanilla pods. (You can wash and dry them and keep them in a jar of sugar, which will give you vanilla-flavoured sugar for use in all your baking.) Cover the surface of the bowl with greaseproof paper straight away to prevent a skin forming. Allow to cool, then store in the fridge until you're ready to use it.

Makes about 300 ml

250 ml full-fat milk

½ vanilla pod

3 egg yolks

40 g caster sugar

Crème anglaise

This is 'English' custard, made without flour, which can be used as an accompaniment, hot or cold, to a warm tart. If you can make crème anglaise, you are halfway to making vanilla ice cream. So if you don't need all of the custard, you can churn it in an ice-cream maker.

Put the milk into a heavy-based saucepan. Using a sharp knife, split the vanilla pod along its length, scrape the seeds into the milk, then put one half of the pod in too. Place over a medium heat and bring to just under the boil.

Put the egg yolks and sugar into a bowl and whisk until pale and creamy. Pour the milk slowly into the egg mixture, whisking well as you do so. Return the mixture to the pan and place over a medium heat. Using a wooden spoon, stir continuously in a figure of eight until the custard thickens enough to coat the back of a spoon. (To test, lift the spoon out of the custard and draw a line down the back of the spoon. If the line stays clean, the custard is ready.) Strain immediately into a clean bowl and continue stirring for a few minutes. (You can wash and dry the halved vanilla pod and keep it in a jar of sugar, along with the unused half of the pod, which will give you vanilla-flavoured sugar for use in all your baking.)

Serve hot, or leave to cool, then store in the fridge, covered with cling film, until you're ready to use it.

200 ml full-fat milk

1 vanilla pod

2 egg yolks

60 g sugar

20 g flour

100 ml double cream

Crème légère

This is a beautiful, classical cream that is halfway between crème patissière and chantilly cream. I call it an 'ambient ice cream', which is, of course, a contradiction in terms, but it has all the flavour of a great vanilla ice cream without being frozen. You make the base in the same way as crème patissière, let it become cold, then whisk in some double cream so that you end up with something that is less dense than crème patissière, but more substantial than chantilly cream. It is also a fantastic way of stretching some crème patissière that you have left over. Use it instead of crème patissière as a base for fruit tarts or tartlets (see pages 105), in Mille-feuilles (see page 171) or Chouquettes (see page 192), or substitute it for the chantilly cream to make swans' feathers (see page 181). It is also perfect for dipping strawberries into. A big bowl of berries, a bowl of crème légère, some little Shortbread or Langues de chat biscuits (see pages 143 and 147) and a glass of dessert wine at the end of a summer evening: beautiful!

Put the milk into a heavy-based saucepan. Using a sharp knife, split the vanilla pod along its length, scrape the seeds into the milk, then put the pod halves in too.

Put the egg yolks and sugar into a bowl and whisk until pale and creamy. Add the flour and mix until smooth.

Put the pan of milk over a medium heat, bring to just under the boil then slowly pour half of it into the egg mixture, whisking well as you do so. Add the remainder of the milk and whisk again, then pour the mixture back into the pan. Bring to the boil, whisking all the time, then keep boiling and whisking continuously for 1 minute. Take off the heat.

Pour the mixture into a clean bowl and scoop out the vanilla pod. (You can wash and dry the vanilla pod and keep it in a jar of sugar, along with the unused half of the pod, which will give you vanilla-flavoured sugar for use in all your baking.) Cover the surface of the bowl with greaseproof paper straight away to prevent a skin forming. Allow to cool, then store in the fridge until you're ready to use it.

Whisk the double cream until thick and fluffy. Whisk the cold crème patissière, then mix in the double cream with a wooden spoon.

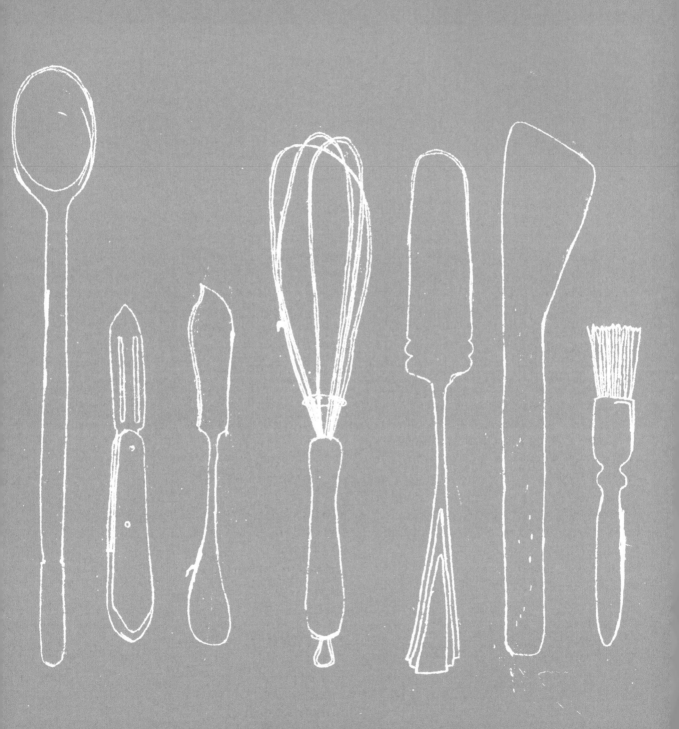

Suppliers

Equipment

Pastry-making doesn't need much in the way of specialist equipment but you will need a few things.

For bowls, rolling pins, whisks, pastry brushes, cooling racks, tins, cutters and cases, we have a selection at The Bertinet Kitchen:

The Bertinet Kitchen
12 St Andrew's Terrace,
Bath,
BA1 2QR
www.thebertinetkitchen.com

There are many good independent kitchenware shops around. Seek yours out. Ones we have used and love include:

Kitchens, Bath, Bristol & Cardiff
www.kitchencookshop.co.uk

Kitchener, Cheltenham
www.kitchenercookware.com

Kitchen Ideas, London
70 Westbourne Grove, Bayswater
London, W2 5SH

Food

CHOCOLATE

Divine
www.divinechocolate.com

Green & Black's
www.greenandblacksdirect.com

Melt
www.meltchocolates.com

CREAM, MILK & CHEESE

Ivy House Farm (milk & cream)
www.ivyhousefarmdairy.co.uk

Neal's Yard Dairy (cheese)
www.nealsyarddairy.co.uk

Trethowan's Dairy (cheese)
www.trethowansdairy.co.uk

FISH & SHELLFISH

The Scallop Shell
Beckington, nr Frome, Somerset
www.thescallopshell.co.uk

FLOUR

FWP Matthews
www.fwpmatthews.co.uk

Shipton Mill
www.shipton-mill.com

GAME

Everleigh Farm Shop
www.everleighfarmshop.co.uk

HERBS & SPICES

Seasoned Pioneers
www.seasonedpioneers.co.uk

MEAT
Use your local butcher. Ours are:

Terry & Son, London Street, Bath

Bartlett & Sons, Green Street, Bath
www.bartlettandsons.co.uk

RAPESEED OIL

Fussels
www.fusselsfinefoods.co.uk/

R-Oil
www.r-oil.co.uk

READY-MADE PUFF PASTRY

Dorset Pastry
www.dorsetpastry.co.uk

SALT

Cornish Sea Salt
www.cornishseasalt.co.uk

Halen Mon
www.halenmon.com

SPECIALITY GLAZES

The Fine Food Company
www.finefoodco.co.uk

Online resources

To hone your pastry skills and watch videos of Richard making the sweet, puff and choux pastries, visit his website at:

www.bertinetkitchen.com/videos

You can also watch Richard use the sweet pastry to make a fruit tart (a large version of the Fruit Tartlets recipe on page 105) and the choux pastry to make Swans (see pages 181–187).

And to follow the steps in the book for making the pastries as Richard talks you through them turn to the relevant sections:

Salted/Sweet: pages 16–27

Puff: pages 44–55

Choux: pages 56–59

Index

A

almond
   amandine 118–21
   cream 118–21
   croustillants 176–7
   and hazelnut pastry 17
   Italian biscuits 144–5
   pastry 17
   peach and rosemary tarts 122–5
amandine 118–21
apple
   compote 160–1
   and custard 'leftovers' 168–9
   presentation tips 203
   tarte normande 130–1
   tarte tatin 162–4
   tarts 160–1, 203
apricot
   jam glaze 205
   tart 158–9

B

bacon
   leek and reblochon tarts 68
   slices 150–1
baking beans 37–8, 40, 42
baking stones 37

banana, presentation tips 204
béchamel sauce 150–1
beetroot toppings, for duck pie 80–3
biscuits
   boxful of sweet 138–47
   Breton 142
   everyday 140
   Italian 144–5
   langues de chat 146–7
   orange and chocolate 141
   shortbread 143
   spelt 100–1
blackcurrant cheesecakes 116–17
blind baking 37–42
   12-hole tins 42
   loose-bottomed tins and rings 38–41
Bourdaloue, pear 126–7
Breton biscuits 142
butter, working with 15, 18–21, 48–50

C

caraway pastry 16
chantilly cream 181, 186
cheese
   bacon, leek and reblochon tart 68
   puffs 193
cheesecakes

blackcurrant 116–17
lemon 116–17
mascarpone 116–17
passion fruit 116–17
cherry chocolate tart 110–13
chicken and tarragon tarts 74–5
chocolate
    cherry tart 110–13
    churros 194–5
    crème patissière 208
    éclairs 188–91
    fondant 110–13
    glaze 188–9
    and orange biscuits 141
    pastry 17
chorizo bites 152–3
chouquettes 192
choux pastry 9, 10, 56–61
    basic recipe 56–9
    cheese puffs 193
    chocolate éclairs 188–91
    chouquettes 192
    churros 194–5
    freezing 63
    piping 61, 181–3, 188
    recipes 56–9, 178–95
    storing 63
    swans 180–7
chuck steak, Cornish pasties 78–9
churros 194–5
coffee crème patissière 209
compote, apple 160–1
Cornish pasties 16, 78–9
cream
    almond 118–21
    alternatives 206–11
    chantilly 181, 186
cream desserts
    chocolate éclairs 188–91
    swans 180–7
crème anglaise 210
crème légère 211
crème patissière

chocolate 208
coffee 209
traditional 105–6
croustillants 176–7
currant, white, and rhubarb tarts 128–9
custard
    and apple 'leftovers' 168–9
    tarts, Portuguese (natas) 172–3

D

dill and smoked salmon tart 68
'double book' 44, 53
duck pie 80–3

E

éclairs, chocolate 188–91
egg glazes 40
everyday biscuits 140

F

finishing touches 196–211
    alternative creams 207–11
    apples 203
    chocolate crème patissière 208
    coffee crème patissière 209
    crème anglaise 210
    crème légère 211
    glazing 205
    mixed fresh fruit tarts 204
    raspberries 201
    stone fruit 202
    strawberries 200
flours 15
fondant, chocolate 110–13
food mixers 26–7
frangipane mince pies 136–7
freezing pastry 63, 119
fruit tartlets 105–7
fruit tarts 204

G

galette des rois 165–7
glazes
    apricot 205
    chocolate 188–9
    egg 40
    poaching syrup glaze 122–5

H

hazelnut and almond pastry 17
hot-water crust pastry 85–97

I

Italian biscuits 144–5

J

jelly
    for duck pie 80–3
    for pork pies 85, 96, 98–9
    traditional pork pie 98–9

K

kiwis, presentation tips 204

L

Langues de chat 146–7
leek, reblochon and bacon tarts 68
lemon
    cheesecakes 116–17
    langues de chat 146–7
    meringue tartlets 113–15
    pastry 17
    tarts 108–9

M

mascarpone cheesecake 116–17
measures 12
meringue tartlets, lemon 113–15
millefeuilles 170–1
mince pies, frangipane 136–7
mushroom
    slices 150–1
    and spinach tart 68

N

natas (Portuguese custard tarts) 172–3

O

onion tartlets 71
open tart (savoury) 72–3
orange
    and chocolate biscuits 141
    langues de chat 146–7
    presentation tips 204
oven thermometers 13
ovens 13, 37

P

palmiers 174–5
parsley and smoked salmon tart 68
passion fruit cheesecakes 116–17
pasties, Cornish 16, 78–9
peach and rosemary almond tarts
    122–5
pear Bourdaloue 126–7
pies
    duck 80–3
    frangipane mince 136–7
    pork 84–99
piping bag techniques 61, 181–3, 188
pistachio
    croustillants 176–7

pastry 17

    and raspberry tarts 134–5

poppy seeds, croustillants 176–7

pork

    duck pie 80–3

    pies 84–99

    sausage rolls 154–7

prune and rum tarts 132–3

puff pastry 9, 10

    apple and custard 'leftovers' 168–9

    apple tarts 160–1

    apricot tart 158–9

    bacon or mushroom slices 150–1

    basic recipe 44–55

    chorizo bites 152–3

    croustillants 176–7

    'double book' 44, 53

    freezing 63

    galette des rois 165–7

    millefeuilles 170–1

    natas 172–3

    palmiers 174–5

    recipes 44–55, 148–77

    resting 46

    sausage rolls 154–7

    'single turns' 44, 55

    storing 63

    tarte tatin 162–4

    'turns' 44, 53, 55

pumpkin and ricotta tarts 76–7

R

raspberry

    and pistachio tarts 134–5

    presentation tips 201

reblochon, bacon and leek tarts 68

resting pastry 29, 46

rhubarb and white currant tarts 128–9

ricotta and pumpkin tarts 76–7

rolling out 30–1

rosemary and peach almond tarts 122–5

rum and prune tarts 132–3

S

salmon, smoked, and parsley (or dill) tart 68

salted pastry 8–10, 15–43

    baking blind 37–42

    basic recipe 16, 18–27

    basic recipe variations 16

    chicken and tarragon tarts 74–5

    Cornish pasties 78–9

    duck pie 80–3

    with a food mixer 26–7

    freezing 63

    hand-made 18–27

    heating the oven 37

    hot-water crust pastry 85–97

    lining tart tins/rings 33–6

    onion tartlets 71

    open tart 72–3

    pork pies 84–99

    preparing tart tins/rings 29

    pumpkin and ricotta tarts 76–7

    recipes 16, 18–27, 64–101

    resting 29

    rolling out 30–1

    savoury tarts 66–70

    spelt biscuits 100–1

    storing 63

sauce, béchamel 150–1

sausage rolls 154–7

semolina pastry 16

sesame seeds, croustillants 176–7

shortbread 143

skirt, Cornish pasties 78–9

slices

    bacon 150–1

    mushroom 150–1

'soggy bottoms', tips to avoid 37

spelt

    biscuits 100–1

    pastry 16

spinach and mushroom tart 68

stone fruit, presentation tips 202

storing pastry 63, 119
strawberry
    fruit tartlets 105–7, 200
    presentation tips 200, 204
swans 180–7
sweet pastry 8–10, 15–43
    amandine 118–21
    baking blind 37–42
    basic recipe 17, 18–27
    basic recipe variations 17
    boxful of sweet biscuits 138–47
    chocolate cherry tart 110–13
    with a food mixer 26–7
    frangipane mince pies 136–7
    freezing 63, 119
    fruit tartlets 105–7
    hand-made 18–27
    heating the oven 37
    lemon meringue tartlets 113–15
    lemon tarts 108–9
    lining tart tins/rings 33–6
    mascarpone cheesecake 116–17
    peach and rosemary almond tarts 122–5
    pear Bourdaloue 126–7
    preparing tart tins/rings 29
    prune and rum tarts 132–3
    raspberry and pistachio tarts 134–5
    recipes 17, 18–27, 102–47
    resting 29
    rhubarb and white currant tarts 128–9
    rolling out 30–1
    storing 63, 119
    tarte normande 130–1
syrup glaze, poaching 122–5

T

tarragon and chicken tart 74–5
tart tins/rings
    baking blind with 12-hole tins 42
    baking blind with loose-bottomed 38–41
    choosing 29
    lining 33–6

    preparation 29
tarte normande 130–1
tarte tatin 162–4
tartlets
    fruit 105–7
    lemon meringue 113–15
    onion 71
tarts
    amandine 118–21
    apple 160–1, 203
    apricot 158–9
    bacon, leek and reblochon 68
    chicken and tarragon 74–5
    chocolate cherry 110–13
    lemon 108–9
    mixed fresh fruit 204
    mushroom and spinach 68
    natas (Portuguese custard tarts) 172–3
    open (savoury) 72–3
    peach and rosemary almond 122–5
    pear Bourdaloue 126–7
    prune and rum 132–3
    pumpkin and ricotta 76–7
    raspberry and pistachio 134–5
    rhubarb and white currant 128–9
    savoury 66–70
    smoked salmon and parsley (or dill) 68
    stone fruit 202
    strawberry 200
    tarte normande 130–1
    tarte tatin 162–4
traiteurs 64
'turns' (puff pastry) 44, 53, 55

W

weights and measures 12
white currant and rhubarb tarts 128–9
wholemeal pastry 16

For my beautiful family and chief tasters: Jo, Jack, Tom and Lola Maude

Acknowledgements

This book has been written amidst a year of change and development for our business. I am hugely indebted to the whole team particularly Debbie, Carrie and Sarah, and my bakers Kieron, Brett, John, Mark & Will who make many of the pastries in this book daily.

A huge thank you to Sheila Keating for her unfailing ability to transform my words into wonderfully readable text; to Imogen for her drive and vision to give this book a home; to Carey, Sarah, Ed, Katie, Rae, Alice and all at Ebury for their support and for 'getting it'; to Jean Cazals for the beautiful photographs – surely another award for you within these pages Jean! To Will for the design and layout; Trish Burgess for her copyediting; Charlotte for her fantastic drawings and lovely handwriting; and to Jess for her work on the recipes and during the shoots. Finally, thank you to Jo – my rock and the best friend, wife and mother to my brood I could wish for, without whom the show would not stay on the road.

10 9 8 7 6 5 4 3

Published in 2012 by Ebury Press, an imprint of Ebury Publishing

A Random House Group Company

The Random House Group Limited Reg. No. 954009

Addresses for companies within the Random House Group can be found at www.randomhouse.co.uk

A CIP catalogue record for this book is available from the British Library

The Random House Group Limited supports The Forest Stewardship Council® (FSC®), the
leading international forest-certification organisation. Our books carrying the FSC label are
printed on FSC®-certified paper. FSC is the only forest-certification scheme supported by the
leading environmental organisations, including Greenpeace. Our paper procurement policy
can be found at www.randomhouse.co.uk/environment

To buy books by your favourite authors and register for offers visit www.randomhouse.co.uk

Printed and bound in by Firmengruppe APPL, aprinta druck, Wemding, Germany

Design: Will Webb
Photography: Jean Cazals
Illustrations: Charlotte Farmer
Prop styling: Jessica Georgiades

ISBN 9780091943479